STRUGGLING FOR ONE AMERICA

STRUGGLING FOR ONE AMERICA

Trump vs. Hollywood:
The Two White Houses

DAPHNE BARAK &
ERBIL GUNASTI

Skyhorse Publishing

Skyhorse Publishing books may be purchased in bulk at special discounts for sales promotion, corporate gifts, fund-raising, or educational purposes. Special editions can also be created to specifications. For details, contact the Special Sales Department, Skyhorse Publishing, 307 West 36th Street, 11th Floor, New York, NY 10018 or info@skyhorsepublishing.com.

Skyhorse® and Skyhorse Publishing® are registered trademarks of Skyhorse Publishing, Inc.®, a Delaware corporation.

Visit our website at www.skyhorsepublishing.com.

10 9 8 7 6 5 4 3 2 1

Library of Congress Cataloging-in-Publication Data is available on file.

Cover design by Radoslav Iliev and Brian Peterson

Print ISBN: 978-1-5107-6808-6
Ebook ISBN: 978-1-5107-6841-3

Printed in the United States of America

For the memory of Sevim Gunasti
September 4, 1934–August 14, 2020

Contents

Preface

On September 17, 1862, more than twenty thousand soldiers were killed or wounded in the Battle of Antietam, the bloodiest day in American history. All told, 750 thousand soldiers died during the American Civil War from 1861 to 1865. That would translate into about 7.5 million US deaths in proportion to America's current population. *Struggling for One America* is written with those in mind who lost their lives because America was then divided on the emancipation of the enslaved people.

***

Since the 2016 presidential campaigns, conservatives, liberals, Democrats, Republicans, whites, and non-whites in America began lauding that they are "fighting for America." Yet, by the 2020 presidential election, they were even more divided than united despite all the good intentions of most. Now that America is well into 2021, it is time to yearn for "One America" but without fighting.

***

Here is the caveat—to achieve "One America," the "Trump phenomena" must first be understood. Next, discrimination and racism in America must be revisited. After that, "cancel culture" and "No-No rhetoric" must be handled promptly and sensitively. Finally, Hollywood must first embrace the #MeToo movement and then come up with a long-term strategy.

For that reason, director Daphne Barak and producer Erbil Gunasti brought on board twenty-four Hollywood stars and entertainers in their *Trump vs. Hollywood* documentary. Half were pro-Trump and half against. Daphne interviewed them, posing the question: "Can we talk?"

Struggling for One America stands as the genesis of this documentary. On November 4, 2020, this documentary was revised with a reference to the American Civil War. It is now called *Trump vs. Hollywood: The Two White Houses.*

During the American Civil War, there were two White Houses in America for four years, when unimaginable atrocities were committed by humankind.

This book, in that respect, points at the presumptive and pretended "culprits" and "scapegoats" in the current divide, while focusing on the obvious. Nowadays, the two White Houses are standing tall, in plain sight. A step further in the wrong direction from this moment on would be nothing less than repeating history.

Introduction

Struggling for One America: Trump vs. Hollywood: The Two White Houses is book number eight attributed to two authors: It is the seventh for Daphne Barak and fourth for Erbil Gunasti.

The book is a culmination of a documentary project. It involves Donald J. Trump, the forty-fifth president of the sole superpower in the world, and Hollywood stars and entertainers.

***

Daphne writes in this book as the interviewer of the stars and entertainers in the documentary, in first person singular. She fills in in real time what transpired all throughout with anecdotes.

Erbil writes in third person plural, as the producer of the documentary that was observing what transpired before his eyes. He also narrates the book to put it into perspective how both authors viewed the developments during filming for the documentary and writing this book to present a larger picture to the reader.

***

Filming sit-down exclusives with A-listers is a domain Daphne has been traveling in for more than two decades. She has interviewed hundreds of inaccessible leaders, Hollywood superstars, and many others with global name recognition for decades.

The US network televisions aired them. The leading print outlets in all major media markets around the world, including the US, printed them. They generated cover stories and top ratings.

***

Daphne is well known for her first book, *Saving Amy*. It is about the six months Daphne and Erbil spent with Amy Winehouse and her parents.

That was three years before Amy's passing, during the twenty-seventh year of her short but very memorable life. This encounter also produced the *only* interview with Amy before her passing.

Amy was quoted in *People* magazine, "Only Daphne Barak can explain my complicated life," when the book was released in London in 2009.

It is also important to note Daphne and Erbil are the reason why Amy went to St. Lucia and stayed there for four months, but also why she returned back to London only two weeks after their week-long visit with her.

***

Daphne and Erbil have collaborated on two other books. In addition, while Erbil edited Daphne's earlier books, Daphne also contributed to a chapter in Erbil's book, *GameChanger*.

***

Coming Home with the Kennedys was one project they worked on together, which included photographs taken by Erbil during their historic trip to New Ross, Ireland. Daphne and Erbil were exclusively in the company of thirty-five members of the Kennedy family, led by Caroline, the daughter of John F. Kennedy, the thirty-fifth president of the US. The ceremonial week in June 2013 was to commemorate the fiftieth anniversary of JFK visiting his roots for the first time.

Their other joint project involved a cookbook. It was called *Mama Sarah Obama: Home Cooking Recipes*. The recipes belonged to the paternal grandmother of the forty-fourth president of the USA, Barack H. Obama Jr. Daphne and Erbil cooked each one of these dishes at their home in California together with the Obamas while the book was penned alongside an autobiography.

***

The autobiography *Mama Sarah Obama: Our Dreams and Roots* and *My Benazir* are the other two books by Daphne.

My Benazir refers to Benazir Bhutto, two-time prime minister of Pakistan. She was murdered in a second suicide bombing attempt during an election campaign in Rawalpindi, Pakistan, racing for a third term in office.

Daphne and Erbil spent lot of private time with Benazir and her husband, Asif Ali Zardari, until her assassination in 2007. They were in exile, living in Dubai and New York, respectively. Daphne was in constant touch with both of them for two years before Benazir's murder.

She was on the phone with Benazir only a few hours before her passing. More importantly, she was also on the phone with her husband Asif. Asif called Daphne repeatedly right before and immediately after the assassination.

Mama Sarah Obama: Our Dreams and Roots is the autobiography of the paternal grandmother of President Barack Obama. Daphne and Erbil visited her twice at her home in Kogelo, Kenya. It is a little village near the Uganda border, what Kenyans call "Up Country." To you and me, it is deep in Black Africa.

Though she passed away in March 2021, visiting this (at the time) very healthy grandma was an adventure, considering she lived in such an isolated little village. To get there, they had to fly into the third-largest city of the country, Kisumu, near Victoria Lake. The second time around, their little chartered plane landed in a banana field, and soldiers emerged from it with a delegation to welcome Daphne formally.

The first visit was equally challenging to say the least in order to reach the soon to become "first Grandma of the US." First, two weeks earlier, Kisumu was in the news. There were riots and about 1,000 people were butchered in the mayhem.

Second, Kogelo, where she lived, was a three-hour drive away from the airport. Traveling the pothole-ridden road to the Uganda border and back had to be completed before sundown for safety reasons. When they returned, it was midnight and airport was shut down.

***

The book itself was written in La Quinta, California, where Obamas from Kenya spent time as guests of Daphne and Erbil in their country club home. Daphne wrote the book from the voice of Mama Sarah Obama, focusing solely on Barack H. Obama Sr., father of the forty-fourth president of the United States of America.

In the book, she explained the relationship between a hugely talented son and the woman who raised him. A cookbook became the by-product of this project as they enjoyed all the food they ate together during the long journey.

***

Daphne's sixth book was *To Plea or Not to Plea*, published in 2020. It is based on filmed interviews with political consultant Rick Gates when he was being investigated for the "Russia collusion" by the Special Counsel Robert Mueller and his team.

A quote from one of the world's most renowned editors of a major daily in London, explains it best how Daphne Barak is considered a scooper that marvels the pros in the field: "Only you could have found yourself in this position, at the very center of a story which all the world is fighting for . . . and only you could have coped so well."

Although this editor was referring to yet another Daphne Barak work, involving a scoop Daphne pulled during the passing of Michael Jackson (MJ), it is nonetheless fitting. Daphne spent time with Rick Gates when he was toxic, meaning no one dared to talk to him in order not to be subpoenaed by the special counsel. In MJ's case, Daphne and Erbil were with the long time nanny of his children Prince, Paris and Blanket when the sad news of his passing was announced in 2009.

Daphne already had the scoop everybody was trying to get about MJ's kids on the day of his passing from her, same as when Rick Gates was with all the answers regarding the fate of the forty-fifth president of the US.

***

Daphne's partner in crime, Erbil Gunasti, a.k.a. "Bill" but also "Mayor Gunasti," came up with his first book *GameChanger: Trump Card: Turkey & Erdogan* in 2020.

Apparently, Erbil had some spare time. He had been simultaneously writing it while he was working with Daphne filming for the book with Rick Gates. *GameChanger* is published in the US and Australia. It is also being published in Turkey and Japan.

GameChanger points to the Muslim migration and argues unless the USA and the Republic of Turkey work together, Western Civilization in Europe as we know it will be in jeopardy from demographic changes.

The book also focuses on the forty-fifth president of the US, Donald J. Trump, and Recep Tayyip Erdoğan, still the president of Turkey. The two nationalist leaders started working well together in late 2018 and both presidents publicly acknowledged the book and congratulated Erbil for the job well done.

***

The authors have been GOP delegates at both the 2016 and 2020 Republican National Conventions. They started supporting Trump's candidacy in June 2015 and they were with him all throughout his presidency.

Daphne has been a lifelong liberal. She supported both Clinton and Obama candidacies for the 2008 and 2012 races. She also hosted them and their family members at home.

As Hillary Clinton said when she was their guest for a fundraiser in 2004, attended by a hundred fat cats and Hollywood celebrities and entertainers, "Everybody has a six-degree separation, Daphne has zero!"

President Trump also said to First Lady Melania, "If there is one person who can do it in America, it is Daphne." He was referring to the biggest scoops Daphne aired on US network television primetime shows.

***

Daphne and Erbil produced their *Trump vs. Hollywood* documentary in 2020. They filmed it with twenty-four Hollywood stars and entertainers during the COVID-19 pandemic in America. They released it a couple of weeks before the November 3, 2020, presidential election.

On November 4, they decided to revise the beginning of it to adjust to new realities. They called it *Trump vs. Hollywood: The Two White Houses*.

When the opportunity was offered to publish a book on how the documentary was made, they took the challenge.

They decided to focus on moments with President Trump after filming, as well as important times they spent in the White House after November 3.

Sincere conversations in trying to create a dialogue between "Two Americas" became the focal point, because by then filmmakers were already *Struggling for One America*.

CHAPTER ONE

The Journey

_____

At the beginning,
We had **Fighting for America** in mind.

Then we decided,
it had to be **Struggling for One America.**

We concluded:
Everybody in America was **Fighting for America**
and they were **dividing** America more and more.

That was not right, and something had to be done.
So, we brought twenty-four celebs from opposing sides and inquired:
"CAN WE TALK?"

*S*truggling for One America was developed long after the *Trump vs. Hollywood* documentary idea came to fruition. Daphne Barak and Erbil Gunasti, the director and the producer of the documentary, always believed in "One America." As naturalized citizens, they decided to be part of the political process to fulfill a civic duty.

Soon, they witnessed to their horror that the presidential campaign was becoming a fight to the bitter end in 2016. Yet, they still had faith, like most Americans, that the system in

America was the best in the world and it was going to overcome and heal the differences.

When Donald J. Trump was elected as the forty-fifth president of the United States of America, they thought there would be a new beginning. Winning against all odds, coming from behind, was the American way. Trump had done it with "American Spirit."

In America, the republic was built on the premise that you earned when you worked hard. The "survival of the fittest" was one of the main pillars most everybody adhered to.

Yet, what took place from then on was nothing promising. By 2019, "One America" was a bridge too far, but worse, at a closer look, the bridge was not even there. The divide was too big and there was no way to bridge the gap.

***

On November 8, 2016, Daphne and Erbil got an early morning phone call from America. They had just arrived in Israel late that night. They were feeling relieved that the election was over, not knowing who had won the race.

It had been too much to bear since June 2015 when they first committed to candidate Trump. By now, like the majority in America, maybe they too had resigned to the obvious: Hillary Clinton had won the race.

No, it was not so! Their candidate was victorious. The phone call was from Jeff Stone, one of the senior state senators from California. He gave them the news with elation.

***

When they arrived back home, they found a new reality. They were two of the 1,237 delegates dedicated to the new president and took part in formally registering his presidency. Now, they were part of history.

Still, they had no sense of urgency. Not until receiving another phone call inviting them to Washington, DC. It was the beginning of a new journey for them that would also take them golfing in Florida . . . but not before a "Japanese Twist" that will take them yet to another unknown in the Far East.

Soon, they were going to be yearning to say: "California Here I Come." Now they were spending so much time in the East Coast. *Trump vs. Hollywood*-type projects were coming into play and they directly involved the forty-fifth president of the USA.

American Spirit

Daphne and Erbil became Trump delegates with American Spirit.

They thought to fulfill this citizenship role by becoming part of the political process. Yet, supporting a very vocal underdog like Donald J. Trump as early as June 2015 was considered insane by lots of people.

All the while, there was also growing number of others who admired the spirit they were displaying for the sake of a process that is so dear to every citizen of this superpower.

The fact that Daphne, a lifelong liberal, was registering as a Republican delegate dedicated to candidate Trump was fascinating. Someone who earned a living from Hollywood choosing to brave such a divisive political process deserved an explanation but also respect.

Erbil, on the other hand, had already run for mayor of Palm Springs as soon as he became eligible as a newly minted naturalized US citizen, was nothing short of a lofty display of loyalty to the Republic. Never mind the fact that he ran to represent LGBTQ-heavy Palm Springs, where seven other candidates were Democrats.

***

George Washington is considered the embodiment of the American Spirit, without a doubt. He never wavered in the face of a challenge.

Thomas Jefferson, the nation's third president, also infused the American Spirit with a new ideal: the notion that citizens can achieve greater opportunity, and equality, through learning.

Daphne and Erbil Never Wavered

The director and the producer of the *Trump vs. Hollywood* documentary never wavered in the face of toxic political process or the COVID-19 pandemic. Their American Spirit reflected on dozens of Hollywood stars and entertainers that they included in the project.

The task of getting a voluminous group of inaccessible, talented, resourceful, and accomplished elite of the society was an extraordinary effort. Yet, they were not disappointed. The prospects came out in hordes with "spirit," so to speak.

Practically, none of them was talking to that point beyond the bubble they were living in. To build everything on a simple premise was yet another aspect of this accomplishment. Posing the question "Can we talk?" was at the least forcing the very issue at hand.

Hollywood Stars and Entertainers Also Came Out in Hordes

Simply put, it was a challenge for each one of these Hollywood stars and entertainers to join this call. Some of the Trump loyalists did not know who else was going to be part of the project. The rest did not know what the others had already said.

When all was said and done, the comments included in the documentary from Kid Rock, Andrea Bocelli, and Robert DeNiro were crystal clear. Each raised a high point with emphasis but also with emotion. They represented American pride, the esteemed place of the White House in the world, and the voice of Hollywood, respectively.

What Scott Baio, Dean Cain, Isaiah Washington, Kristy Swanson, Robert Davi, Kevin Sorbo, Sam Sorbo, and Ted Nugent brought forward was frank and to the point. This was an opportunity to state the facts openly and effectively.

Eric Roberts, Eliza Roberts, Avi Lerner, and Mark Geragos did not shy away from what they thought was right and wrong. They explained their point of view directly. Lorenzo Lamas complemented the documentary with his perspective.

Eric B, Too Short, Money B, Glen "Big Baby" Davis, DeRay Davis, and Claudia Jordan proudly and objectively stood their ground. By then, the number of those that did not waver was already close to thirty. However, the documentary included just two dozen of them.

Learning Was For Everyone

Scott, Dean, Isaiah, and Kristy learned that they were the first four to sit down with Daphne and must be given credit for being brave. Robert Davi, Kevin and Sam Sorbo, and Ted Nugent did not need encouragement; they were living within the spirit of Thomas Jefferson: learning, equality, and opportunity.

Eric, Eliza, Mark, and Avi sat down with Daphne, representing Hollywood liberals. They immediately noticed the documentary was preaching equality and providing an opportunity to balance the point of views. Yet, they were there to express the facts as they saw them and how they experienced them.

Plus, it was no secret to them that Daphne had been part of Hollywood for decades. She had spent time with many legends, had interviewed lot of them, had earned their respect along the way, and built an impeccable reputation.

African Americans Left Their Marks

When African Americans joined the project, the filmmakers had already learned a lot about the fears and anxieties of a good number of American elite. At that stage, they were not conscious of the spirit of George Washington and Thomas Jefferson.

After all, as far as they were concerned, *Trump vs. Hollywood* was not intended as a project to educate. Yet, since they were filming in real time, they were constantly learning. Now they were facing a bunch yet to tell their side of the story.

Who Else Did Not Waver But Also Learned?

Donald Trump and Hillary Clinton had both shown great determination to win the presidential race in 2016. Neither wavered. So when the results came, they continued with the same "spirit." Neither was relenting.

Losing was not an option. Yet, this was a presidential election. One side had to win for the process to continue. Somehow, the "other side" never wavered in 2016. Similarly, in the next presidential election, when the "other side" won in 2020, the losing side returned the favor and continued not to waver.

***

In the previous elections, when Barack Obama had won against all odds, it was different. Defeated Americans then had accepted the results and respected the forty-fourth president and stomached the change that he brought to the country.

No one could have predicted that in 2016 the division in the country would continue and after 2020 it would even become worse, considering the outgoing president never conceded.

Did anyone learn anything from 2016 and 2020 presidential races in America?

The Documentary Was Filmed with American Spirit

Nonetheless, *Trump vs. Hollywood* was filmed and edited with the American Spirit of learning and never wavering. Participating

Hollywood stars and entertainers reflected that in their spirit as well.

Yet, when the project was completed, America was at a crossroads. So, the filmmakers decided to make a revision at the beginning of the documentary. They added a historical footnote with reference to the Civil War of 1861 to 1865.

Now, they were posing yet an additional question, as if history was repeating itself. Like then, there seemed to be the prospect of the two White Houses in sight for this American Spirit to ponder. And the questions could only be answered with a book to put everything into a perspective.

Golfing in Florida

Golfing was not part of life for Daphne and Erbil until recently, even though they had residences in two of the most desired country clubs in California, each with 18 holes. For them, they were only nicely trimmed, secure, and peaceful grounds—the perfect places to work, especially when isolating became mandatory with COVID-19.

***

Meanwhile, in Palm Beach, Florida, membership in this club seemed to require a Rolls Royce. In some cases, his and hers were customary. Surely, the display of wealth was no different than other well-to-do country clubs across America.

Except here, everything was in your face. There were so many Rolls Royces around that the assumption was easy to make. Like the Jet Set of the 1950s that were required to have their own plane, the wealth here had its own denomination with a Rolls or two.

***

For President Trump, it was golfing that was the most important. He was in Florida regularly for that and hosting visitors at the same time in an informal setting. Invited guests were regulars and there was a waiting list for the privilege.

Lunch was the main event after the golfing round, next to the gala dinners. Daphne and Erbil would be invited to take their place next to the "First Table."

President Trump valued these private exchanges and the opportunity to get information or opinions directly. In one of their private chats, he asked Daphne to whisper in his ear, aware that people were watching from other tables and trying to read her lips.

Conceived on Thanksgiving, 2019

It was late November 2019, where Bill and I celebrated Thanksgiving at Mar-a-Lago with friends. We were seated at a very desired long table, just next to the one reserved for President Donald Trump, with gold stanchion posts and red velvet rope around it.

Though the setting was a routine every night for the first couple, this had been one of the most "in demand" evenings at Mar-a-Lago since Trump had become president. And guests were competing for nearby tables with the president.

Beside eye contact with him, or a wave, it showed how many "connections" these guests had. No, not with the president. Actually, with the well-tipped club employees, but the optics managed to impress some.

That evening, the self-service buffet was as rich as the year before. Guests measured each other's jewelry. Only the main player was missing—Donald Trump had slipped out of his "Winter White House" the day before, after playing golf, as usual.

He would fly sixteen hours to join our troops in Afghanistan. The trip was kept secret until it was safe to share it with the public the following day.

So, the usual presidential table was headed by Melania Trump. She was joined by her parents and members of the Trump family.

The next day, we were scheduled to have lunch at the Trump International Club with friends. I was not surprised to see the secret service there; yes, Trump headed to his beloved golf course, right after returning from Afghanistan.

I went to say "Hi" when he took his usual break for lunch. We chatted about our mutual friend, actor Jon Voight. Trump always reminds me, "Tell Jon how wonderful he is!"

I said something to the effect that it is not easy (for Jon or others) to support Trump in Hollywood.

He looked at me and asked, "Why won't you film with these actors? They should talk about it." Is that the moment the film, *Trump vs. Hollywood*, as well as this book, was conceived?

Donald Trump: Daphne Barak Business

No one could have guessed that what began that day as a project between Daphne and the forty-fifth President of the United States would be evolving and enduring. It was simply supposed to be a documentary called *Trump vs. Hollywood*, talking about mundane things at best by famous supporters of the president.

By the time the idea culminated into a book, the Civil War had already become "Close Encounters of the Third Kind" as the main thesis. What had begun as an informative exchange, inquiring if the two sides could talk, was now looming as an all-out atrocious moment in history no one wanted to remember, never mind experience again.

Meanwhile, with the turn of events on November 4, 2020, the documentary took its final form and was renamed: *Trump vs. Hollywood: The Two White Houses*. Now, it focused on what had long become the real problem of America: a split in society much like what may have taken place prior to the Civil War that gave way to the atrocities from 1861 to 1865.

***

Daphne had been involved in another equally monumental "war" of a sort in the past. It was between Donald and Ivana Trump and it was taking place everywhere.

Daphne had already become part of this duel by interviewing Ivana during their divorce case, which was followed globally. After that, she had also interviewed Donald. For her, giving equal access was the right thing to do.

Daphne was a dominant international interviewer in those days. She was airing highly rated sit-down interviews with Hollywood stars, heads of state or government, royals, and others with global name recognition. She was also syndicated in the leading print and broadcast outlets of all major media markets around the world.

***

Now, with Erbil, both as Trump delegates, authors, and documentary filmmakers, they could not have sat idle. There was a split in America and they had direct access to both sides. Daphne was known to have the "president's ear" in close circles. She also had great friendships and, more importantly, a good reputation in Hollywood.

Daphne had a saying: "If we cannot have lunch with an interviewee after we filmed and aired the interview, we did not do the right thing." With that motto, she garnered the biggest ratings and elevated the legacy of some the world's biggest names including Princess Diana, Amy Winehouse, Benazir Bhutto, and Michael Jackson.

President Trump, with First Lady Melania and Erbil present, once turned to his wife and said: "You may not know but Daphne made the biggest rating in television history." The first lady said that she knew what he was talking about and concurred. [Note: Daphne's *Our Son: Michael Jackson* reached one billion viewers within forty-eight hours in fifty-three countries, premiering on ABC Television's *20/20*. It was produced with Elisabeth Murdoch.]

Was This Film Conceived in January 2017?

While preparations for the Trump inaugurations were taking place, rumors were flying about several well-known artists who refused what has been considered as "a great honor" to appear at the inauguration.

Bocelli's Life Was Threatened

Andrea Bocelli was one of those names floating around, as he was considering performing. He knew Trump. He had told me before how thrilled he had been to visit the White House (during President Bill Clinton's administration).

I was chatting with his wife Veronica. Bill and I had produced a special about their love story, *Maestro at Home*, an "ICONS in their own words with Daphne Barak" documentary series. I recalled his respect for our national symbols like the White House.

Veronica shared with me that nothing was confirmed in regard to the inauguration, and that there were other considerations. She sounded stressed about the rumors. And indeed, on January 14, 2017, Bocelli backed out of the Trump' s inauguration because he was receiving death threats, including some against their young daughter.

Rick Gates Concurs

Rick Gates was the deputy campaign chairman and a member of the inauguration committee. He told me on camera, exclusively, how insane the situation was. There were not only threats to boycott Bocelli's performances, but also actual physical threats on him and his family.

I was not even sure what Bocelli's political views were. Having met Andrea and Veronica Bocelli's youngest daughter, and their united family, it was a painful account for me to digest. It has stayed in the back of my mind as a troubling reminder.

Almost New Year: Roseanne Barr

Right after Christmas 2019, Bill and I were again in Palm Beach. Bill's foreign policy book, *GameChanger: Trump Card: Turkey & Erdogan*, was about to be published in the US and key markets overseas. We had an advance copy from one of our publishers, and we stopped for lunch at the Trump International Club.

The local papers posted on their front pages that actress Roseanne Barr would be receiving an award along with me at an event in Mar-a-Lago at the beginning of 2020.

Being ousted from the ABC series carrying her name has been too horrific for her to put it behind and move forward. Whatever she did wrong, she immediately apologized for. She thought she had been a target before her fatal nightly tweets.

Trump, not a stranger to "tweet controversies," supported her, tweeting that Hollywood had double standards. He mentioned how actress Debra Messing was not fired by NBC for tweeting to blacklist his supporters, while Roseanne was fired by ABC.

Trump and I were chatting when he asked John Nieporte, his golf trainer, to give me his mobile number and coordinate our private meeting with Roseanne. Trump then congratulated Bill publicly for his book, engaged in a longer conversation, and accepted a copy of the book.

The following day, he said, "There are other people in Hollywood who are hurt because they are supporting me. Maybe you would like to find out more?"

It became clear to me: Jon Voight and Roseanne Barr had already talked publicly about their support of President Trump. But what about others? Would they go public? If so, would they be candid about their reasons to voice their support of Trump, their timing, their painful moments? Maybe even funny moments? What is it like to be a Trump supporter in liberal Hollywood?

Jon was in the same state of (gallant) mind: "You guys find about as many others. Everybody knows where I stand. I have already talked enough."

He shared some names and joined us for a couple of dinners or chatted with us over the phone while filming. We filmed a couple of the interviews at his studio, shared with his partner Steven Paul. Steven was also super supportive of this ambitious film.

We lined up names of those we wanted to talk to about "Trump vs. Hollywood."

California, Here I Come

It is a long way back to California. So, does contemplating what transpired in Florida.

Since New Year's Eve in 2016, Daphne and Erbil have been bicoastal, spending every other week on either cost. So, they started to play with the idea of the documentary.

Bringing conservatives on board was one thing but getting them "out of the closet," so to speak, was another, and a gigantic task.

On the other hand, the idea of making a documentary with only three heavyweights was also intriguing. Yet, it never made sense when it came down to the message. Nothing that they would have said would have made headlines because there was no controversy. Plus, they had voiced their opinions loud and clear on many platforms.

The problem at hand was that America was divided, not that America did not know where it stood. So, appealing to One America made sense as opposed to "talking in the submarine," like Daphne would often say.

They finally thought, what if they had many conservatives coming out of woodwork? What would they have? Especially if those conservatives had not voiced their opinions yet, or shared them enough times on social media.

Maybe they had differences of opinion or maybe they were all on the same page, reflecting how rigid the divide actually was.

On the other hand, liberals could also have had the same unity or division within. Until they were posed the question, and enough of them answered, the temperature could not be determined.

Then came the question of where to find all these Hollywood stars and entertainers in the first place.

Where else but in California? Rather, in Hollywood itself. In reality, it was Los Angeles, or better yet Beverly Hills. It is not for nothing "California, Here I Come" had become a coined phrase for lots of people in America and across the world in search of celebrities.

So, going home to California was the right thing to do. The project had to start there. Yet, first things first: they had to decide on the casting agent.

Casting for Trump vs. Hollywood: Blessing or Curse?

Jill Thacker, our casting director, jumped in with much energy. Weeks later, she would admit how sensitive this assignment would become.

Bettina Viviano, a conservative producer and a lovely figure, helped with a couple of casting decisions, and shared her tearful tale of her experience in Hollywood since she announced she was a conservative.

It looked like we were going into production. The direction of the documentary was clear. Bill and I and our team booked Hollywood players and some musicians who were Trump supporters.

Yet, I also included other key voices, like our friend, top Hollywood attorney Mark Geragos, who represented the likes of Chris Brown, Wynona Ryder, Colin Kaepernick, and many others. Geragos is a very vocal anti-Trump advocate.

Another friend of ours, mega producer Avi Lerner, was also included. Avi, like me, long supported the Clintons and Obamas. But in the 2016 presidential election Bill and I supported Trump, while Avi supported Hillary Clinton. I figured he would talk the anti-Trump lingo. Well, things would become interesting.

We also included Eric Roberts, the brother of *Pretty Woman* Julia Roberts and father of Emma Roberts. Eric, known as "the hardest working man in showbiz," would not disappoint. Some of his anti-Trump rhetoric became "headlines," even in a polarized Trump era.

Brett Ratner, a Hollywood director who was responsible for such mega hits as *Rush*, was included as well. He has not worked in Hollywood for a while, like others accused in the era of (mostly justified) #MeToo.

Our interaction with Brett would become way more interesting, time consuming, and literally sweatier than expected. Not to mention the mega media interest about him! And even more disturbing legal actions were uncovered by the media, weeks after we filmed with him.

All was ready to go. Then, suddenly, a big dark cloud spread over all of us: COVID-19. The production was delayed, as we needed to reset and make responsible decisions. A few weeks later, we started a safe and restricted production protocol.

Washington, DC, Mandate

In Washington, DC, President Donald J. Trump and his team, headed by Vice President Mike Pence, were the basis of COVID-19 protocol for the federal government. Very soon, they concluded that states had equal say in this life-and-death situation that was currently engulfing the great republic.

The protocol from Washington was summarized on the blue and white pamphlet. It was identifying the rules of engagement during COVID-19 and it was voluntary advice. It was also realistic because like Daphne and Erbil would soon find out, the circumstances and conditions were different in each state.

Yet, politics was also in play. In New York and California, there were ordinances from local authorities. They were making the rules, which were very conservative, restrictive, and interfered in daily life. In Florida and Texas, the announcements were symbolic, informative, and practically nothing was mandatory.

In other words, there were two Americas. The two most liberal states were acting very conservative in the face of pandemic, while the two most conservative states were most liberal when they came to the liberty of the individuals.

Washington, DC, was a story on its own. It was nothing like those four states and the rules there were extraordinary. Sometimes, they were brutal. Other times, life was beautiful.

***

Daphne and Erbil, though, were operating on a simple premise from the perspective of producing original content. There was a Republican administration in the federal government and it had issued a pamphlet for guidance.

So, it had to be observed and followed. In the states, the authority was local, so they had to abide by their rules. They simply had to respect that end of the spectrum.

Their experience in Washington up to that moment was serving them well. They had learned and adapted to the culture there. When George Floyd died in the hands of police in Minnesota and COVID-19 descended like a black cloud, nothing changed for them. Despite being affected deeply, they adapted and continued with the mandate deep down in their hearts and minds.

Being Part of the Culture in the Making

Daphne and Erbil first arrived at Trump's Washington on New Year's Eve in 2016. When balloons started to come down, there was a festive atmosphere.

They did not know then that the Trump International Hotel in Washington, DC, was going to be added to their stable of "home away from home." The hotel had first opened its doors in September 2016. By 2019, they had been living in the hotel for two years. During the journey, they joined friends and colleagues when they came visiting Washington.

Mornings in the lobby of this historical building were always bright. If not sun, daylight was piercing through. It used to be the main US post office, but somehow it was refurbished and modernized right in time for the Trump presidency.

For Erbil, mornings in the hotel meant a chocolate croissant and Coffee Mocha. For Daphne, it was specially squeezed juice and Coffee Latte. That was their routine.

Then, there were friends and bureaucrats from the federal government, as well as members of the US Congress. They often joined them there in the afterhours and in the evenings.

Soon, many others were also migrating to this hotel, which was becoming like a shrine. Over the next four years, this place became the only other location in Washington, DC, that President Trump would visit outside the White House.

***

Daphne and Erbil first thought that "Trump vs. Hollywood" would be a good way to put everything into perspective. Yet it wasn't until they embarked on this journey that they would realize just how big the divide in America was and that it would not be a fair portrayal if the other side was not represented.

When they came up with *The Two White Houses* version of the documentary, they were reflecting the reality at hand after the November 3, 2020, presidential election.

Now, there were existential threats to the republic. One was the pandemic and the other was overtaking everything when the George Floyd killing happened.

Suddenly, racism was taking America back to the 1860s. COVID-19 and the issue of racism soon became bigger than President Trump or Hollywood or America itself.

Hence, *Struggling for One America* was no longer a choice but vitally important to reflect the reality at hand, especially when Joe Biden moved into the 1600 Pennsylvania Avenue.

George Floyd Happened: Now Race Was Also the "Faith" of America

When we were halfway through the original filming, George Floyd was killed. The video documenting his cruel killing by a cop, who was kneeling on his neck while George cried for help and called to his late mother, shocked America. It shocked many around the world. It shook me in the deepest way. It went under the skin.

The filming of *Trump vs. Hollywood* would evolve then and there into an inclusive direction. As America evolved in true time, Bill and I invited well-known rappers, sports figures, and actors from the Black community to join the film.

We filmed, dined, listened, engaged, and tried to bridge with the other side—even with Trump! Now, it was becoming more than a Hollywood film. It was becoming America! In real time. All the while, COVID-19 was also continuing with its lasting and widespread effect, like the plague of the modern times.

Covid-19 is an Eternal Damnation

COVID-19 changed lives, possibly forever, but it is important to note when exactly it arrived in 2020, as far as this film and book are concerned. It came just before they began filming; in other words, the documentary itself became purely a COVID-19 project.

When everybody went into quarantine, restricted to homes, the filmmakers went out to do the job. Did it occur to them that the project could have gone down the drain? Apparently, nothing like that came to their minds.

Daphne has always been a go-getter. Nothing had ever stopped her when there was a scoop to get and no one else was able to get it. She had been known to earn the biggest ratings for the US network television prime time shows, time and again.

Now, considering the importance of this project, not even the eternal damnation of COVID-19 was an obstacle for Daphne. Going after only two dozen interviews?

***

Daphne, had conducted interviews in Zimbabwe, Libya, and Cuba with Robert Mugabe, Moammar Gaddafi, and Fidel Castro, respectively. She survived to bring the footage home each time, out of what lots of people would call the ends of the world.

Nothing was too dramatic for Daphne and Erbil to conduct an interview under any circumstance anywhere. Since the Hollywood interviews were within the states, they must have been piece of cake, considering. To put it into perspective, Daphne also went to Pakistan, Kenya, and Georgia for interviews.

Erbil was with her for the last two. In Pakistan, she was there right after a *Wall Street Journal* reporter was butchered with a knife. In Georgia, it was within a few weeks after Russia invaded North Ossetia and tanks were about 30 kilometers from the capital of Tbilisi. They met with the president of the country, his wife, and his mother.

In Kenya, they were there only two weeks after a massacre in which one thousand people perished. Yet, they went "up country" to see the grandma of the forty-fourth president of the US at her home in Kogelo, near the Uganda border.

They always came back with interviews intact. Each episode itself could be a movie and a book. They were dramatic.

The coronavirus was equally dramatic in the US in 2020, as it was for Erbil. In addition to COVID-19, there was the 2020 presidential election. On top of that, Erbil's mother was hospitalized. She was newly transferred to San Diego Scripps after lots of difficulty.

As if COVID-19, family drama, and election-year anxieties were not enough, Daphne and Erbil had planned a voyage to Japan. They had never been there, yet their lives revolved around discovering and indulging, so no matter what the circumstances were, there was no excuse to pass it up.

The urgency to go to Japan in the nick of time is yet another story to tell, but nonetheless, it came like a medicine to the work at hand.

In Japan, they learned a lot about the coronavirus. So, in a sense, they came back prepared to film during the COVID-19 pandemic. Maybe everything was meant to be with the documentary, which led to this book.

In one respect, it was reflective of who they were and what they would do with the documentary as filmmakers. They had a life beyond Washington, DC, and Palm Beach, Florida. Surely, it was going to be reflective of that, no matter how they made it.

For them, life was also in California and Texas, but it also used to be in New York until the pandemic hit. They also had life in Turkey and Israel. They were born there, respectively, and became naturalized Americans after hard work and a long time spent in Turkey and Israel, as well as in Europe.

In that sense, going to Japan explained who they were as filmmakers. Their interest was not limited to just US politics or the Trump revolution that captivated lots of people. They were adamant that they would continue to live their lives as they have always lived them with the rest of the world community.

This double life was giving them an edge in doing their projects that others could not have enjoyed. They were not the kind to stay behind closed doors. They were ready to venture to the unknown anytime, under any circumstances, pandemic or not, wars or not, massacres or not. It was a way of life, no more or no less.

Much like making this documentary and this book.

Japanese Twist

Japan, a close and old society, gave them a couple important pointers before they started filming in the US.

The filmmakers gained something extraordinary from that trip. They learned that Japan was an organized and a clean society by nature. There, they witnessed how to cope with COVID-19.

The Japanese people apparently seemed ready for COVID-19 because they were already wearing masks in their daily lives. It was part of their routine, pandemic or not. They were conscious of what was in the air anytime.

Unlike in the US, where freedom, at times, meant not many boundaries, especially lately. For Japan, existentialism had clear boundaries. In a sense, they were respecting the space of others.

Ironically, that was in clear contrast to the sights of Japanese metro trains packed like sardines. Yet, on this trip, existentialism was most apparent in the restaurants, where patrons sat in isolated and separated quarters.

Their society was compartmentalized. So, when Daphne and Erbil returned to America over the next few months under COVID-19, they were going to benefit from that experience.

***

Basically, they compartmentalized everything like the Japanese were doing and filmed everything without risking anyone catching COVID-19.

They simply "learned" something from the "other side" and applied those lessons for the good of everyone. The whole reason to do this documentary was, like Jefferson would have said, learning to give opportunity?

A Visit to Yokohama: Becoming a Learning Lesson

We were about to go into production when Bill and I were invited for a rather urgent visit to Japan. It had to do with Bill's foreign policy book, which was getting contracts in more markets around the world. Japan was one of them.

It also had to do with private exchanges about what certain Japanese businessmen were facing, financially and image-wise, a few days before their government would be forced to announce that it would postpone the much-anticipated Summer Olympics, due to the spreading pandemic.

Even though COVID-19 was underway, and we were thinking that we would be working fully on the *Trump vs. Hollywood* documentary, life seemed to be continuing uninterrupted when it came to going to Japan.

From our doctor friends in San Diego, Maryam J. Hekmat and Zahra Ghorishi, and their husbands Reza and Sean, we were hearing worrisome voices. They were already so worried about the coronavirus that they were questioning our idea to go to Japan. For us, it was just something we had to do. Nothing was going to interrupt our lives.

In reality, if we did not go to Japan we would still be on airplanes, like we were upon returning to film the documentary in five different states and ten different cities. We jumped on and off airplanes throughout the few months of filming.

In that sense, it was nonsensical for people to be worried that we would be traveling.

In fact, it was peculiar. There was no one at the San Diego International Airport. We were the only passengers, perhaps. The 787 Boeing was empty. We were in first class and there were only a handful passengers on the plane to Tokyo.

On the way back a few days later, the picture was no different. In Tokyo, the airport had a full table of cancelled flights, except for our flight, standing alone.

In San Diego, we took photos. There was only one person in the picture because the other person was taking the photo.

But there was not another soul in the whole airport. It was eerily empty.

Have you ever seen a parking lot in any airport with no cars? It was all empty. It was surreal. Not a soul in Tokyo, same as in San Diego. As if the whole airport and airline were working only for the two of us. Why were we flying while everybody else was secluded at their home? We did not know the answer. It seemed odd that we were conducting business as usual while everybody else was suddenly nowhere to be seen.

What made us to behave like that? What power imprisoned so many, so easily?

We Were Also Living in a Bubble, No Less

COVID-19 was already a fact in the US. Bill's mother, was at a hospital in San Diego, and called for us to come. We rushed there before our flight to Tokyo. That is why we actually booked our flight from San Diego airport, so we could see Bill's mother twice, going and coming.

When we pulled up to the hospital, everything was normal until we arrived at the lobby. There we were told that by the order of the governor the hospital was now closed to visitors. It was like a death sentence. We were on a flight to a destination we had never been, in a pandemic. It was like a last supper to see Bill's mother one last time and bid farewell, so to speak.

California by then was like a state under dictatorial rule. Access was closed. So, we found a nurse on the floor where Bill's mother was and asked her to come down so that we could give her an iPhone to pass on to his mother so we could at least talk to her on FaceTime before the flight.

She was kind enough and as we drove in a hurry to the airport, we made contact and were able to talk to her. (Erbil's mom was instrumental in the making of *Trump vs. Hollywood* and she

passed on August 14, 2020, as the documentary went into editing.) We all felt good. Now we could fly into the blue yonder
without looking back.

Going to Japan was like a journey to a new life, leaving an
elderly father back in the desert, a mother in the hospital, and a
sister to look after both of them in our absence.

It was lot to think about, because we were also leaving two
dogs, Dovey and Miri, who are so dear to us, behind.

They were with Bill's father and sister whenever we flew,
but this time we were going out of the country during unprec-
edented circumstances. So, everything had some melancholy
to it. Separation anxiety at the fullest, thanks to the coronavirus, augmented to levels one can only realize when one
lives it.

COVID-19 made us live it on this Japan trip. So much so
that, for a while until flight took off, we were not even thinking
about why we were going to Japan and leaving our livelihood —
the documentary and family members and dogs —behind. It was
very consuming.

But once we were in the air life began to change as rapidly.
These Japanese were different altogether.

First, they were all wearing masks. At that time, masks were
not yet common, not to mention required, or they were yet to
be enforced.

Only when we arrived in Japan did we understand that the
Japanese wear masks, coronavirus or not, as part of their daily
routines. Apparently, when they say Japan is a clean country that
is what they mean.

The people of Japan were already treating every day as
if there was a pandemic as long as anyone remembers. Oh
boy, was it a lesson we learned, coming back to America few
days later, where everyone was worried or complaining about
masks for no reason.

These Japanese Businessmen

In fact, the idea of going to Japan had come from the other side of the Pacific. These top Japanese businessmen were insisting that we come there as if there was no global emergency. They even scheduled meetings for us with their political leaders. So, we decided to take a short trip to Tokyo. Little did we know, it would be our last overseas trip for a while and America would be locked down upon our return. We boarded the flight, planning to start filming upon our return.

The first-class cabin on our Japan Airlines flight was mostly empty. The hostesses were wearing masks, but nothing else offered a feeling that it might be one of the last normal flights between the US and Japan.

We were greeted by a Japanese senior representative at an empty airport in Tokyo. His bosses were waiting for us in the nearby Yokohama—the power base of Yoshihide Suga, who, we were told discreetly, was about to replace then–Prime Minister Shinzo Abe months later.

It happened, and we were there, in real time, while these historical discussions were taking place.

Arriving to the newest hotel in this nice, quiet city, was the beginning of several fascinating days, before most face-to-face international meetings would cease.

While the US was closing down rapidly, Bill and I were still shopping at the malls, and being treated to nonstop lunches and dinners, while discussing books, films, and visions.

Corona Princess: Here We Come!

One of these dinners would become unforgettable. A top Japanese businessman—a man who controls many businesses at the Yokohama port, decided to host us for dinner on a boat.

When we arrived, we found out that he closed the whole boat for our intimate dinner. But before the food and drinks started to arrive, he insisted on taking us to the boat's deck. The other Japanese members of our small group were getting excited.

They knew what was coming next. Bill and I were led to a deck, when our host clapped hands, and said, "Look behind you!"

Behind us was a lighted cruise ship. "This is IT," he said with an aura of drama. "This is the *Corona Princess*."

That was the *Royal Princess* cruise ship, where several cases of coronavirus were found early on. The ship could not continue its cruise, let alone dock anywhere. Stories of human drama were reported all over the media.

After innocent tourists were stuck in their small cabins, surrounded by a spreading virus, they were rescued at last.

Yet the infected cruise ship was invited nowhere. Therefore, the cruise line had to continue maintaining it at the Yokohama port.

The savvy Japanese, who had not been thrilled about this toxic vehicle in their precious port, realized quickly that they could charge the cruise line a hefty parking fee, plus they could turn the ship into a tourist sensation.

While dining on sushi and then cooked fish, our host was delighted to treat us to another surprise. "I was told that you liked jazz music."

"Love it," I replied.

Our gracious host motioned, and two pretty women walked in with violins.

As they started to play, the curtains behind them opened. The *Corona Princess* ship was revealed, with glitzy lights.

Our boat was sailing, fine wine flowing, nice jazz musicians entertaining us . . . yet the infected corona ship added what *should* have been an ominous background, yet from the point of view of these businessmen, it was seen as "pictorial"; making the best out of a tragic situation.

Time to Go Back Home and Deal with Corona

After a few days in Japan, it was time to go back to the US and start the production of *Trump vs. Hollywood*.

Just before we were taken to the airport, our Japanese new friends told us that "two of the biggest tabloids found about your visit, and are making front page stories about it later this week."

"WHAT??" I asked. I was really lost in translation. Then and there.

How could Bill's book options, film discussions, and private exchanges take over the Japanese agenda of that week?

Well, they did.

With their Olympic Games delayed, their huge efforts to legalize gambling, the power struggle between Yoshihide Suga, Shinzo Abe, and Toshihiro Nikai (the leader of the Democratic party, LDP Shisuikai), a declining economy—suddenly our visit was portrayed as: "glamorous," "powerful," and "secret." Even power brokering between Yokohama's rumored mafia boss.

We boarded our flight back to the US in a totally deserted airport. Apparently, our flight was the only one not cancelled.

COVID-19 already had taken control of both airports. The flight back was almost empty, as well.

But only when we landed in San Diego did we realize how much life has also changed in a few days in the US. The picture was desolate at best.

The airport was dark. No flickering electronic board. No passengers.

Bill captured me watching in bewilderment at the deserted San Diego airport.

I had no idea how we would find our luggage.

Two suitcases greeting us downstairs were a symbol that life had changed! We would need great energy, unity, responsibility, and daily judgment in order to move forward during a deadly pandemic. We had plenty of time to digest the new reality after Japan.

Before that, we would schedule our first interviewee, Scott Baio.

CHAPTER TWO
The Culprits

Scott Baio, Dean Cain, Kristy Swanson, Robert Davi, Kevin and Sam Sorbo, Ted Nugent, Bill Whittle, and PG made the list as Trump loyalists. So did Isaiah Washington.

Half of America was sure to consider them culprits because they were conservatives. Yet, they were also heroes to the other half of America.

Not everyone that became part of this filming was conservative or Republican or pro-Trump. There were also the "Holly-Liberals" that were willing, and rather itching, to talk.

Robert DeNiro and Meryl Streep had become the heroes of the Hollywood-led Globalist community. They were openly using the public platforms with bias against the conservatives.

On the other hand, Eric and Eliza Roberts, Claudia Jordan, Eric B, Money B, Too Short, Glen "Big Baby" Davis, and DeRay Davis found a platform with this documentary. Then there were the likes of Avi Lerner, Mark Geragos, and Brett Ratner in motion pictures. For these three, Israeli, Armenian, and Cuban heritages were justifiable excuses to switch loyalties in and out of Hollywood.

By 2020, America too had become, much like Hollywood, very complicated. Whether they were conservatives or liberals, they were sure to find themselves at the crossfire for wanting to do the right thing for simply trying to speak the truth.

Yet, one thing was clear. In order not to be considered or worse even blamed as a "culprit," one had to be mute, blind, and deaf in America.

For the filmmakers, splitting interviewees into two groups was not the intent from the beginning but starting with conservatives—rather, Trump loyalists—was. Hence, anyone that did not fit into that category was considered by the filmmakers simply as "liberals."

***

Scott was the first brave enough to cross over. He had already done it by speaking from the podium of the GOP convention in Cleveland, Ohio, on behalf of Trump in 2016. He was also the first interviewee for the *Trump vs. Hollywood* documentary.

The filmmakers had to take it one step at a time. Playing safe and going after the obvious was the right thing to do at the early stages. Scott was it until rocker Ted Nugent came on board to put the conservative point of view over the finishing line.

He was the last of the conservatives brought on board, yet he spoke plenty. There was no way to stop him from speaking his mind with all the shotguns, bows, and arrows around at his ranch! As a gun-toting NRA member, his rhetoric was enough to put him in the crosshairs as well as make him a hero, like Donald Trump had become to many.

***

Eric Roberts stood out among the dozen that were against Trump. He was on the cover of *Vanity Fair*. His wife, Eliza, daughter, Emma, and sister Julia all had their accolades from Hollywood. They represented Hollywood royalty.

Yet, Eric was belligerent enough to deserve as much credit as the filmmakers had bestowed on Ted when it came to the "lead culprit" role from the opposing side.

Not that other liberals did not say anything less offensive, but nobody used the rhetoric Eric indulged in. Was he incendiary like Ted or were they only playing their roles and being more vocal than others in this divided America?

***

In the end, everything had to be put into a perspective. Ted was saying, "I have never met a racist person in my life." Eric was countering him with, "We have a lunatic in the White House!"

Wasn't this the same type of incendiary rhetoric in America that once experienced a Civil War over race? Were there two White Houses, soon after, officially designated by half of the population?

Conservatives: Ted Nugent

How could Ted Nugent be right?

> No, he is not a racist. I am convinced that President Trump, like everybody I know, and I know a lot of people, and I know the biggest rednecks in the world. I hunt with them. I track with them. We kill alligators together. We skin things together. Rednecks. I have never met a racist person in my life.
>
> —Ted Nugent

What about hypocrisy?

> I hunt with a bow and arrow. you know how many animals I killed with an arrow? One! You know how many animals a tractor kills preparing your tofu salad? Billions.
>
> —Ted Nugent

After Donald J. Trump became the forty-fifth president, conservatives in America did not have any chance to be right about anything. Ted Nugent was no different. Nothing he said was believable to the liberals.

Daphne and Erbil did not know much about Ted Nugent at first. Ted was the lead guitarist of the Amboy Dukes, a band formed in 1963 that played psychedelic rock and hard rock.

Erbil, coming from French boarding school and Turkish background, and Daphne, from Israel and Northern European influence, had different tendencies. Between themselves, they had more than half a dozen languages and cultures.

Yet, Ted was an eye-opener for them. Meeting him and his wife Shemane at their ranch was quite an experience. They were shooting to kill, eat, and use every piece of what is left over from their kill. They were true conservationists. That was one their first "truths."

Not Knowing What to Expect

Ted Nugent invited us to his three hundred–acre (!) ranch in Texas. COVID-19 made all of us isolate, and a trip to Texas proved itself challenging. We flew our cameraman Tim Carney with us—safety was key!

Hotels had just reopened in Dallas. Our team booked us at Hotel Crescent Court, a lovely property, which was experimenting "baby steps" of opening under coronavirus. We were allowed only two at a time in the hotel's elevators. The cleaning materials were so strong that I developed a rash.

Yet, the Nobu restaurant opened once again. I jumped at the first table available. It gave Bill, Tim, and I an opportunity to bond again with Bettina Viviano and her hubby, Jimmie, and try to fake "normality."

Yet, first came work!

Ted's team led us through his rural big ranch. It was not that well taken care of; that was the beauty of it. Mother Nature.

Ted appeared at the door of a house, wearing shorts, smiling. Then, a beautiful blond with a welcoming smile followed: Shemane Nugent, Ted's soft-spoken wife.

Their house was a real piece of conversation! Dead animals on the walls and floors. Shemane told us, "I killed the zebra [on the floor] with an arrow."

OUCH! Now, Ted does not take prisoners.

He is there, in your face, weighing it out, as he sees it. And he does see many things other people miss or leave aside. Ted Nugent expresses his observations bluntly. And I had to admit, after the initial shock, that he did do his homework about "being a conservative." One may disagree with him, but Ted's arguments are challenging.

***

After a tsunami-style interview, Shemane took us to see the new house at the property. It was still under construction. The water system was self-sufficient, as was the entire concept.

She told me, "I learned how to do manicures myself. We are just here inherency. Who would drive an hour to give me a manicure?" Their food and drinks were all self-sustained.

Shemane had asked my team if I would agree to grant an interview for her podcast. I could never decline such a warm invitation. So, we settled on her sofa at the "new house" and taped her segment, but not before she asked, "Daphne, was Ted too much? I was a bit worried, looking at you, when you interviewed him."

"No," I said, "Ted knows his stuff, and his convictions are worth listening to."

I also observed the sensitivity of being "being Ted Nugent's wife." Not many could pull that off. Shemane Nugent does it. Lovingly.

Welcome to My Ranch

Ted Nugent: I like to see wildlife. I like to see birds and the deer and the squirrels. So, before corona, I am a free man. I would like to meet the man that would come up to me and tell me, "Ted, I have decided you cannot spill corn on your property." In Michigan, they dare to decree that. I could go on and on. There are a hundred examples. Michigan government has lost its soul. And it is a direct manifestation of a cultural deprivation that metastasized from California and New York, the liberal hell hellhole, Democrat, censorship, oath violating, and you cannot keep or bear arms in New York or New Jersey or Maryland or Massachusetts or Illinois. So, I have witnessed the incremental chipping away at the most self-evident truth. Basic freedoms and individual rights, as our founding fathers wrote down, in the Constitution of the Bill of Rights. And even had they not been written down; I think you already know what those rights are.

I am just a guitar player, but in my heart, I know I have the right to speak my mind. I do not need a document to give me that, right. I do not need another man to go, "Oh, by the way, Ted, you can say what you like." Shut up, I will say what I like, whether you authorized it or not. I can choose my own religion. I do not need authorization for that. I can be secure in my papers and in my home. I do not need anybody to authorize my security, my privacy. I can assemble with my fellow human beings and protest violations or instinctual rights. I do not need the First Amendment to give me those rights. But it is nice that our founding fathers wrote it down so that somebody wanted to play king again. If somebody wanted to play tiger or emperor in the United States of America, we can knock him back.

So, the same thing goes for the Second Amendment. I do not need the Second Amendment to keep and bear arms. God gave me that, right? The founding fathers just happened to write it down because no society could have these basic freedoms. And now they are being chipped away. And I will summarize it in the inescapable and obvious evidence of what has happened in the Second Amendment. As an American, I have the First Amendment. And guess how many states have the First Amendment, fifty? What happened to the second one? I do not have the right . . . . I do because I am a sworn sheriff deputy, but it does not say anything about being a sworn shift deputy to have a right to keep or bear arms in fifty states. So, we saw this incremental chipping away at our instinctual God-given individual rights as outlined in those secret documents. So, I became an activist because I saw that some man thought he had authority over me, when it comes to those basic freedoms, and I am not buying it.

You want to play Concord Bridge; I will meet you there at two o'clock. And if you need me to interpret that, I will be happy to. But I have been a hell-raiser because the founding fathers wanted every American to be suspicious of bureaucracies and government. They wanted us to demand constitutional accountability from our elected employees. And until Donald Trump came along, an outsider who identified the vote Garrity of the status quo, runaway train of censorship and freedom elimination. And that is why we voted for this guy because he was not presidential. Because all those presidential guys were scammers, oath violators, and criminally corrupt in their abuse of power. And we needed a Donald Trump to come in and start cleaning the house otherwise known as a draining the swamp. So, I would love to know.

I Am for the Second Amendment, Bush, and Trump

Well, I helped get George Bush elected because there was a governor in Texas named Ann Richards, who ended up being exposed and going on a date with Mario Cuomo, the poster boyfriend [of] liberalism and censorship and violating individual rights in New York.

And I knew that is what she was made from. I liked your [countenance]. I am a big fan of cocky. I am a big fan of leadership when its benefits quality-of-life erring on the side of individual freedoms. Ann Richards was exposed. And we are going back to the Second Amendment again. After twenty-three innocent lives were lost in Luby's Cafeteria because Texas did not allow you to keep and bear arms. Daphne, Texas, remember the Alamo, Texas, you could not keep and bear arms. Now the Texans will tell you I got one in my truck. Well, everybody who died at Luby's Cafeteria [Killeen, Texas] had one in their truck.

But they were [forbidden] to have them on their person, which is keeping and bearing. And they all perished at the evil democracy of [a man named George] Hennard. Punk named Hennard, who literally walked up to Texans and talked to them before he brains up. And they were all forced into unarmed helplessness by the Ann Richards status quo. Punks that weasel their way into positions of authority. And Texans, I am going to have a heart attack. Texans obeyed that bitch, and they did not keep and bear. By the way if your guns [are] in the truck, you are not keeping and bearing, you are keeping, and trucking and they did not have time to get to them.

Living Within Your Means

Trucking. And every instance where an innocent life is lost is because some tyrant punk said, "I've decided you can't keep, and you can't bear arms." And people accepted it.

The violations of our Second Amendment are the indicator of incremental loss of individual rights throughout the recent history of this country. Now, remember I was born in 1948, so I was just breast-stroking in the afterglow of that American GI, driven by individual freedoms to come home [for] dinner. The only place with individual freedom, so they fought more tenaciously, more ferociously, and they defeated the evil Japanese Emperor punks and the Nazi punks, and the whole world looked to America. So, I was born lucky, lucky guy.

I was born at a time where Les Paul electrified the guitar, Chuck Berry showed us what to do with it. And we defeated the evil Japs and Nazis, and the American dream was about earning your own way, busting your ass to be the best that you can be, living within your means and saving for a rainy day.

What the hell happened? You know what, earning your own way means getting get up early and busting your ass. Living within your means does not include tobacco, alcohol, meth, fentanyl, tattoos, body piercings, or bling.

So, I was raised in a disciplined time, where, at the end of the day, you had to be honest with yourself. Have I remained in the asset column today for my family? And all my friends in Michigan were like that. All my friends across the country, I am lucky because I know everybody in America, I rock and roll every state. I hunt in every state. I travel all over the world and I understand people because when they come up to me, Daphne, they are uninhibited. They let me know exactly what they think, good, bad, or ugly.

Daphne: And it all adds up.

Ted: And it adds up. So, if I sound like I know something, it is not because I am smart, it is because I pay attention. And so being clean and sober all my life, I can absorb accurate information so I can gauge my cause and effect, my activities. Does it hurt other people? Does it compromise their American dream, or does it assist with their American dream and make things better for the people around me?

I am expressing not the Nugent philosophy, but the self-evident truth that makes America so wonderful. And everybody that voted for Donald Trump lives, this positive, productive samurai, I hate to even reference a Japanese indicator, but samurai means the best that you can be, applied to positive function, positive effort so that you are not only taking care of yourself and your loved ones, but everybody around you benefits. And you go to bed at night, I go to bed at night with a little . . . grin on my face, knowing I took care of my wife and dog, my sons and my daughter and the grandkids, my brothers, my sisters, my neighbors, the land, the wildlife, the guitar.

And it unleashes my musical soundtrack that literally represents that. And I have got the indicators by the thousands of heroes of the military that play my songs when they are going into battle to fortify their warrior spirits. It is their words, not my words.

You might notice I have some purple hearts around here. I did not earn those. They were given to me over all these years, Vietnam, Desert Storm, one guy from World War II gave me one. None of them knew each other and they all said the same thing, they handed it to me, and I resisted, but you cannot resist a Navy Seal.

And they all said the same thing, "Ted, I want you to have this because you fight for all the freedoms my buddies died for."

So how could I not have confidence that I might be on a good cause? So, when I speak, I represent the heartbeat of those Americans that voted for Donald Trump. That he represents those of us that make sacrifices and take risks to be in the asset column, to be a benefit to the world. As goes America, I think goes the world in many ways.

When Trump Announced

When he came down that escalator with Melania, I said, a politician and I did not know him well. I knew he was an entrepreneur. I know he was a successful . . . when you only see him in the media. Because they print and they must put out a universally loved approach. I saw that he did not put out a universally loved approach.

He was tough. He was street smart. When Shemane and I met him at the rally, he fortified that assumption. He was cordial and we were shooting the breeze backstage and hanging out and talking about it, because his sons are hunters, and his sons are gun guys. We are talking about my relationship with Eric and Donald Jr. in the conservation lifestyle, the outdoor lifestyle, and the dangers of a Hillary Clinton presidency. He had to cross some bridges that Republicans had failed across in the past, mostly with the union guys, with the Democrat-controlled UAW and AFL-CIO and all of them. They had, over the years, become weak and puppet-like and just obeyed their leaders, until we convinced them and showed them the evidence that their leaders were ripping them off. Now it is obvious cause they are going to jail now. *Hoffa* was not a fantasy film. It was a documentary.

Being a Detroit guy, I must have respect for the union guys because they make America work. They are hard workers, and they are great guys, and they are my hunting buddies. I mean, I hang with these guys, but they were being brow beat, they were being brainwashed. Just robotically pulling that "D" lever every time.

I went on a wallpaper carpet bomb media blitz that ranted and raved about how the unions were being scammed. Those union guys believe in God, family, and company. They believe in hunting rights and private property rights. They believe in taking home what they earn. They do not believe in the government stealing our income to give to Planned Parenthood to perform an atrocity that we are against and donating to candidates that also represent policies that we are against. That is an example that is widespread.

My media, I scolded . . . This is something that a lot of people are not aware of, but they are about to be. I am a hunter. They know. I was organic before it became hip. Venison is the ultimate benefit not just your body, but your spirit, and of the land. That is how you balance the herd and make sure the air, soil, and water can be produced, by managed habitat. Duh.

I would scold what I believe, Daphne, is the largest, most powerful voting army in America that has not shown up yet. That is the licensed hunting families of this country, Michigan, Wisconsin, and Pennsylvania. Michigan, Wisconsin . . . Hmm. How did he win? Michigan, Wisconsin, Pennsylvania. How? He got the union voters, and he got the hunting license voters of those top three hunting states to finally vote their God, family, country consciousness.

Campaigning For Trump on November 6, 2016

Daphne: It was Michigan, right, that you were with him on November 6th?

Ted: Yep. Right till three in the morning.

Daphne: Just few hours before the election, right? When everybody is thinking he is going to lose, and you are with him. What is your personal recollection?

Ted: I am a down-to-earth guy. I am simple. When I play guitar, I play the primal scream that Chuck Berry and Bo Diddley taught us and invented quite honestly in a musical way. I watched the polls. I would look at the polls and go, "Hillary up by double digits?" I was just in Detroit and there was ten thousand people going wild like I just played "Stranglehold" as an encore. Hillary doesn't even show up because she can't draw anybody. I am seeing the reality and then I am seeing the fake news polls. I am going, "This is awesome." The electricity, the energy, the spirit, the patriotism at those events for then-candidate Donald Trump. How do you get a poll that is polar extreme opposite to what we are witnessing?

It was not just by Michigan events with the candidate Trump. I saw it everywhere he went, because he was a non-politician and America was looking for someone to change course. They all saw what Obama had done. Even though he had a miraculous speech and campaign, saying all the right stuff, and then he turned on everything he said, and he did just the opposite. Barack Obama was a gift to America. Because he was so dishonest and such a scam artist, such a racist, identifying people by color of skin instead of content of character, we sat back and went, "How can he get away with this? How can the people who claim to be against racism embrace the definition of racism?" We are all going . . . "He sounded so good. Somebody wrote a great speech for this."

We saw the deception, we saw the dishonesty, and what I saw on the ground with then-candidate Trump has been proven to be an accurate representation of the God, family, country conservative vote in America. And we pray to God every day that it happens again.

Did He Look like a Loser?

I am not a spectator. Again, his demeanor, his casual, comfortable, unprotected, unfiltered dialog and comments were something that you would find at deer camp.

Suppose if I went to bars and played poker, that is where you would find that . . . an openness. Well, here is the clincher, I am a high energy guy. I mean, people roast marshmallows on the flames coming out of my ass when I am on tour, is that legal?

Clean and Sober

I have been clean and sober, so I am in good shape. I eat venison and I am active, and I am a rancher, and I am a tree climber, and I am a mechanic. And I am alive.

Trump makes me look like [Haas 00:01:43], and I love Haas, but he came that night in Grand Rapids. I think somebody said it was his sixth stop of the day. And he was late and did not get in until after midnight, in fact they kept telling me, "Hey Ted, keep the crowd going. He's not going to be here for a while."

So, I was on stage. And of course, I could not have been more comfortable, because if they were there for a Trump rally or were Nugent team members, I guarantee that. Plus, even if you are not a Nugent team member, people of every imaginable persuasion and ideology, if they love great music, I have at least that connection. And so, I am up there with my guitar and I am playing some songs that they all recognize and mouthing off, saying things that no politician or MC at a political rally would ever say, and that is what Michigan expected from me and they knew I would deliver that at a Trump rally by me being totally honest and unfiltered myself.

I kept it PG-13, but still, I did not mince any words. And we really had that crowd going, but Daphne, he did not get in there. I mean, it could not have been before 1:00 a.m. if I am not mistaken, it was late. I was tired cause it is hunting season and I am usually in bed by ten o'clock.

But I was pumped up. My adrenaline was on Whitewater rapids. And when he came in, after doing all those events all over the country, this guy was cocked, locked, and ready to rock, Doc. He was as upbeat as I was four hours earlier. So that proved to me that he is passionate because he was running on adrenaline, had to be, and that he saw the threats against our country, and he loved our country enough to make those sacrifices and call upon an inner samurai warrior spirit to connect with these people that stayed up late to see him in Grand Rapids and all around the country.

So even though it was only incidental, in a couple of encounters with him, both were so consistent in his energy, his sincerity, and again, I was fooled by Barack Obama because he said great stuff during his inauguration, I am going, man, this could be great. This guy is saying, we believe him, he is referencing accountability and individual rights and work ethic and secure borders. He is saying all the things that he completely turned on as his presidency went on. But I could tell that Trump was easygoing. Again, I use the word shit-kicker. He was not trying to impress anybody. He talked to me about little things, like guitar tones and his dog.

Trump Talked "Guitar" With Me

Well, he knew that I was a guitar wrangler, and he goes, "You know, I was raised on that same Chuck Berry stuff so I understand that but how did you ever get asked about my origins with Motown," which are pillars of musical authority worldwide. And I am in that vortex and that is my inspiration.

Obviously, his team had researched me a little bit and they saw the nasty lies and hate leveled at me and was able to get over that. He saw that what the *Huffington Post* said about me was just a nasty lie. He saw that what the *New York Times* said about me was just a nasty lie. And he still was proud to stand shoulder to shoulder with me.

And that proved to me that this was a man who was anything but political. This was a man that was anything but interested in trying to impress someone by playing a Mitt Romney groomed game and taught how to speak by Mr. Rogers or some monotone scam artist. I could just tell that he cared that he represented the heart and soul of the best families. And again, I know some people have hardships in life and why good people must face tougher challenges.

There are means so that we can help those that experience hardship. That is the new America I live. I do not want the government to take care of people in hard ways, because they will waste money doing it, and they will not even get to the ones that really need the help. But your neighbor and your family and the church and the charity, we know who needs help and whether they are just scamming us or whether they just need a brief assistance. A hand up instead of a handout. Just the dialogue that we had, I am going, "This guy is one of us, man. This guy is unguarded, there is no pretentiousness. This guy wants to make America great, and he's actually got an outline of how to do it." And in my lifetime, I have seen liberal policies destroy this, and I saw Trump had an answer to that.

I can see how the healthcare scam was politicized by Obama, and how he had an answer to that. So, it is about pragmatism. A good leader of a household will know how to take care of his house and his family. He seemed to have those instinctual talents and understandings that my brother and my sister and my band and my crew and my dean and everybody in my life, my sons, and my daughters, he was talking our language. And not as a Nugent selfish thing, but as a Nugent giving thing. That he was celebrating those who are in the asset column while being conscious of those in the liability column, how to help them out of the liability column or punish them for intentionally sitting in the liability column. There is a difference between the two.

"Racist? I Have Never Met a Racist . . ."

How about the bastardization of that term? I mean, they called Candace Owens a racist. No, he is not a racist. I am convinced that President Trump, like everybody I know, everybody I know, and I know a lot of people, and I know the biggest rednecks in the world. I hunt with them. I track with them. We kill alligators together. We skin things together. Rednecks. I have never met a racist person in my life.

Never once. And I was down in Georgia and Alabama and Mississippi in 1966, 1967. And I was aware of its existence because I think there was still white-only water fountains. Now being a mushy brain teenager, I did not understand any of that. I did not know what the words Jim Crow meant. I did not know what segregation was. When I saw those things, it was my first exposure to a color reference, but I was so maniacal in my vortex of touring and rock and roll that I pleasantly dismissed those harsh conditions because I was so focused on the next gig, the next song, the next recording, the next city, booking the next hotel. But slowly but surely, I came to realize, when I started hearing about lynching. I was in Detroit during the '67 riots and I started to see the manifestation of race relation failures.

So, I am aware of it because I lived through it. Not during the Emancipation Proclamation, but when racism was still horrific. Never met a racist. I mean, redneck vermin trappers from Alabama, they do not give a damn what color you are. If I need this box moved over there, I just need a guy who can lift that box and move it over there. I had a black bass player; I had a Hispanic bass player. We always adored our black heroes. I have done tours that I called Black Power to show reference to Chuck Berry and Bo Diddley and Little Richard and B. B. King and Freddie King and Albert King and James Brown and Wilson Pickett and the Motown Funk Brothers. These are the gods of musical authority that my circle of music, not just a musician, but music lovers and music fans, that is that was my world.

If there was racism, it is because we preferred black artists. Because Pat Boone did not quite cut the mustard next to Little Richard, but we did not blame him for the color of his skin. We did not even attribute his favorites to the color of his skin. So no, I have never met a racist and I have spent time with Donald Trump, and he is the anti-racist. I am anti-racist. Never judge by anything except content of character, integrity, reliability, and honesty. I could care less whether you are confused about your gender or are black or white or yellow or red. In fact, my heroes were either black or red. I mean my bow hunting lifestyle is about Cochise and Crazy Horse . . . Geronimo. I have a deep spiritual reference for those original bowmen, those original conservationists. And musically, I do not have any white heroes. Well, Mitch Ryder is my hero, but you tell him he is white.

I mean this, in quality of life comes from my black musical God heroes, and my Native American conservation heroes. So, they have always called me a racist. But that is their go-to last-ditch effort. If they cannot debate you, you are a racist. In fact, I believe that in the new Webster's dictionary, the definition of racist is someone disagrees with a liberal. So, it is a shame. It is a shame it is turned into that.

It is intellectually bankrupt, and it is an extension of the fake news. I mean, everybody in the fake news. Racist this. If you disagree, you are a racist. If you reference a condition, without any reference to color of anything, you are a racist. So, it is a shame because if you really wanted to fight racism, you would have to make sure that you focused on real racism, and this whole horrible condition we are witnessing now with the looting and the rioting, and with subjects attacking the police and the police defending their lives.

They do not defend their lives against the color of skin. They defend their lives against a dangerous threat. So, we are living the pain and suffering of a Barack Obama who literally said that because Trayvon Martin was a certain color that it could have been his son. When in fact, Trayvon Martin's mom and dad both kicked him out of the house because of criminal behavior and irresponsible and unaccountable truancy and gang activities. But according to President Barack Obama, he could have been his son because of the color of his skin, not the content of his character. Who could not see that? So, Barack Obama in my lifetime brought race relations to its worst time since the fifties.

Dope and Lies

I think Donald Trump, no man is an island, but I have been so attacked throughout my career because I am against dope, and everybody in my musical world were all dopers. Not all of them, but 99 percent. Instead of just respecting my decision to not drool and puke and die, because that is what dope does to you.

Yeah, some of them claim it does not but they have done so much they did not see that. Comfortably numb is uncomfortably dumb, as far as I am concerned. Nobody's mother says I am proud of Johnny because he is high. Who do you want high? Your children's school bus driver? Would you like your pilot to be high? How about your dentist? Who stoned brings improved quality of life to anyone or anybody? Well, okay. Richard Pryor when he was . . . . All right. I like my comedians. I like my comedians high. They can smoke dope if they have an Uber driver.

I have seen dopers and substance abuse in all its forms ruin everything. I was telling your husband Bill earlier that I turned down dope from Jimi Hendrix, and I said, "You know this stuff's going to kill you, man?" Keith Moon made fun of me because I would not drink his whiskey. "This stuff's going to kill you, man." Bon Scott made fun of me because I would not drink his Jack Daniels. I said, "This stuff's going to kill you, man." John Belushi and Dan Aykroyd invited me to their club in Chicago after a concert. Cocaine looked like an outtake from *Scarface*. I said, "John, this stuff's going to kill you, man." I told Sam [Kinison], all this cocaine is going to kill you. He got clean and sober.

Tell Stevie Ray Vaughan this because even though we jammed, I was not able to communicate with him because he was so out of it. But he got clean and sober and of course, Sam Kinison died in a terrible traffic accident and Stevie died in that terrible helicopter crash.

Intoxicants are bad for you, case closed. Scientifically and biologically and spiritually speaking, when you lose control, you are not as good as you were a moment ago, when you had control. So, I have always been demonized by my musical world, the media, they attack me for murdering innocent animals. I guess they did not hear how organic barbecue got to the table. And they always attack me because I am on the board of directors of the NRA and I carry a gun. Well, eating venison is perfect, it is perfect. Self-defense, carrying a gun is perfect.

And they would constantly attack and hate, make up these nasty stories.

Trump Was Cool, Until His Conservative Policies Unveiled

They loved everything about him. They thought it was cool and cute, until they started seeing what his conservative policies would be . . . We knew it was good for America but let me try to explain the Hollywood phenomena of abject glaring hypocrisy. They would ban guns except for their security details. They are against walls, except around their homes.

They want a clean environment. We should hang our wet clothes up on a line because they decree from their private jets. They donate millions of dollars to save animals and then they eat dead stuff every day. Everybody eats dead stuff, even they go to an animal rights event and they drink wine. Maybe you do not know this, a lot of people do not because denial is so comfortable, that glass of wine is responsible for dead snakes, turtles, frogs, voles, shrews, gophers, ground squirrels, birds, coyotes, bobcats, deer hawks, owls, cardinals.

Maybe you do not know this. You know what a vineyard operator does to protect the grapes for that wine, for your animal rights benefit?

He kills everything that gets anywhere near his vineyard because his goal is to grow expensive grapes for you to have a glass of wine. There is no bird or mammal or serpent or amphibian that survives a vineyard, they kill everything. You grasp that, don't you? Now that I have said it, you understand it must be true because the birds come and they want to eat the grapes, the raccoons come, the squirrels. Well, how do you protect grapes? Poison, traps, .22 rifles. I know these vineyard operators, they kill everything.

And how about the guy that eats the tofu salad, "Well, I don't kill stuff. I eat tofu." Okay, hang on a second there, partner, you know about bean fields for your tofu? You see that guy with a big green tractor, but that thing behind it, that is called a disc. And he is going across that field and guess what is in front of that tractor and disc, gophers, ground squirrels, rabbits, pheasant, quail, meadow larks, snakes. You can guess what that disc and plow does, it kills everything. And you certainly know that crows and seagulls follow the tractor, they are eating the dismembered death. So, we are working on your tofu salad, mister, we are working on it, hang with me.

Because if anything dares to come back into that giant bean field, we got a buddy at Monsanto, you know Monsanto? Or in case anything dares to enter your bean field, you just poison the living shit out of it. Isn't it amazing that I have set records on Joe Rogan's podcast and numerous interviews when I say that? Who could contest what I just said? Who could possibly think that what I just said is inaccurate? I have operated tractors and ploughers. I see the birds eating all the dismembered squirrels, and snakes, and turtles. While they are still alive, they are picking at their flesh. Because "I just eat tofu, I don't kill anything." I hunt with a bow and arrow; you know how many animals I killed with an arrow? One! You know how many animals a tractor kills preparing your tofu salad? Billions.

Vanity Fair / Robert De Niro

So, what I am getting at is that I have already experienced the hate of the Hollywood media. Now do I do TV and movies and I get a kick out of it? Sure. Am I looking for attention? Irony, I do not live down here if I am looking for attention. I like to stay home. But when I play my music, I cannot play my music without attention. I know Donald Trump. He could give a rat's ass about attention or acceptance by anybody, unless they stand with him on principle.

Now, is it cute and fun to go to the *Vanity Fair* event and have some big Hollywood stars praise you? I have done it. It is cute. Cute is not important. Cute is just cheap. Cute is a moment of,

"Hey. Yeah. I love your movie. I love your song." Well, that is not meaningful. What is meaningful is, "How have you raised your sons and daughters?" "Did you show up on time to the meeting?" "Did you put your heart and soul into your job?" Showing up at a movie is not that important unless that is your career and that is your art and your gift. But it is not the acting in the Hollywood embracement per se. You know, who is just as important as Robert De Niro? My welder. Because when he welds, it must last, or I can crash my truck.

Being a Star: "Public Interaction Gets to Be a Pain in the Ass . . ."

I have been in movies. And again, I consider it a cute thing because I have priorities. And when I perform in a movie or on a television show, my priority is; be the best that I can be.

So, we have that in common. Because the stars that you mentioned [De Niro, Brad Pitt], they have a professional dedication that should be revered. And we do revere that. However, you know damn well in the world of Hollywood, there is a self-imposed and much love, insulation factor. Many of them have people that do everything for them. All they do is sleep, eat, poop, occasionally have sex and work. They have people that will go get this for them, people that will organize this for them. And there is an insulation factor when you become ultra-wealthy and ultra-admired as a star.

Which is why some great, great stars have died prematurely, because when you insulate yourself . . . I understand it because even as a whatever level celebrity I am, I like to stay home . . . And I like to shake hands, I like to sign autographs. I will never have to deal with as much as a Meryl Streep or a Tom Hanks. They are just making mega, mega identifiable stars.

But I have a reference to that, and it can become grating. You want to avoid it. So, then you insulate yourself even more. Because, you cannot even have a meal without somebody asking for your autograph. So, you either get a back room or the owner of the restaurant, Wolfgang Puck, takes us upstairs. And as you insulate yourself . . . Now follow me on this. I know you respect your elders. But this is a lifetime of observing and participating. Public interaction gets to be a pain in the ass. You cannot be incognito and everybody . . . "This movie, I love this. Oh, you're my hero." Shut the fuck up. I would like to have a bowl of soup.

Now, I am good at that because that is what I say. "I'll sign your autograph on the way out but leave me the fuck alone."

Which is why I love Donald Trump. So, as you further insulate yourself to get away from this discomforting unique celebrity baggage, we all want to be gregarious. I would like to have a conversation. Robert De Niro, he would probably like to talk to that guy.

Liberals: Eric and Eliza Roberts

Some would call it "free speech" when Eric Roberts refers to the then-president as "a lunatic," but in America his opponents would be judged by the "No-No rhetoric" standards if they were to use a similar language on anything "objectionable" that is outside "cancel culture."

> We have a lunatic at the White House!
>
> —Eric Roberts

Eric and Eliza Roberts are part of Hollywood royalty. Eric is the brother of *Pretty Woman* Julia Roberts. They are also the parents of actress Emma Roberts.

Eliza, Eric's wife, appeared in *National Lampoon's Animal House*. Her father helped write the script for *The Way We Were* about a socialist girl Robert Redford's character fell in love with, played by Barbra Streisand.

Eric's career had started with a big promise. Then addictions took over, and Hollywood fell for his sister Julia instead.

***

Yet, Eric has recovered, and acted in so many movies, that *Vanity Fair* magazine put him on its cover, crowning Eric as "the hardest working man in showbiz."

We visited the couple at their home in Los Angeles in the midst of the pandemic. The house is old, with a certain charm.

We were chatting about how Julia Roberts got so excited, the day before, to be interviewing her big hero, Dr. Anthony Fauci.

The pandemic has created new rules, new stars.

Eric and Eliza are no fans of Donald Trump.

As Eliza told me, "We were discussing that if HE won, we should move to New Zealand."

"THAT far away. . ." I giggled.

"Yes," she said.

She was serious.

Eric put it simply: "We have a lunatic at the White House." He said, "May I preface this by saying, asking why are we still talking about this guy? Any dangerous criminal, we should stop paying attention to them. Don't you think?"

"Well," I replied, "He is your president."

"Yeah, he is the president of the United States. That is true."

"Playing Michael Cohen"

I shared with Eric that I watched a hilarious video of him doing an impression of Michael Cohen, Donald Trump's former attorney, who was convicted to serve time in jail.

Eric Roberts: I've been watching him, his last week in freedom, every day, all day. And I was really studying him because it is a fascinating relationship, a fascinating job he had, and he was the henchman. He was the face. He was the guy you had to deal with first. He knows where all the bodies are buried. He knows the answers to all the questions, and he knows Trump's taxes. So, he knows everything. From being the Don Corleone to now being a problem, he is a real problem for Trump, for the Don. He is a big problem.

Yes! I would love to play him. Are you kidding? What a great actor's thing to sink your teeth into because he is probably a great guy. Probably a great guy who is very intelligent, very smart, very witty, very fun, very interesting, very three-dimensional. But he got stuck in being everything for somebody else, being their everything for their business, which he was, is, was. And man, what a story. I cannot wait to see it. And if I can, I want to be in it.

I would love to play Michael Cohen. Are you kidding? That'd be fantastic.

Trump and COVID-19

Art is a fascinating place in our society. Art comes last. Art comes after development, after education. Art comes last. Art, it is educational, but it is also pleasure. It is the last thing that you get. After everything is done in the town, you go to the theatre. After all the work is done, it is the last thing you get, is art. And he has done nothing for the world or the country to set it up. So, the artists can create art because everything is a mess.

You can blame it on the virus, but had we had someone in office who did his job and thought about the people properly, it would have been horrible anyway, but it would not have been as horrible. And we could have pat ourselves on the back, "Thank God we have our stuff together that we don't sink over this. We can survive it." We had to had to catch up. We are catching up and we are doing well, but a lot of people died.

Oh my god. It is insane. And that's so tragic, because hundreds of thousands of people affects half a million of people, instantly. It affects even more than that, but instantly . . . a million people are hurt. It is an awful place we are in. And one of the first things that Donald Trump did was he got rid of the pandemic department, closed it down. Why would you do that?

Why not have it always standing by, since the world, especially the Western world, we are a Petri dish for pandemics. So, we know that. That is a fact. It is not an opinion. So, why did we close on a whole department? It's tragic.

When Hillary Lost, I Went into Depression

I was a Hillary Clinton fan from the word go. I supported her when it was her or Obama. And then when she lost that, I was heartbroken. But I got behind Obama and learned to love him for the right reasons. He was handed the worst debt ever handed an American president. And he survived it. He helped us survive it. Classy, dignified, elegant, smart. Can speak like no one in the twentieth century, this fantastic speaker. I mean, an incredible human.

One of the reasons I hate Donald Trump is how he had bad-mouthed Obama. Had he been handed Obama's debt; what do you think he would have done? We do not know, but it would not have been probably any smarter than what he is doing now.

I remember the night she lost . . . I was absolutely behind Hillary all the way. Then it is him and Hillary. Of course, she is going to win. Of course, there is no contest. He is reality TV star who inherited a bunch of money. Okay. It is okay. He is entertaining. And suddenly she lost the election. It was such a short thing that it is like being told you have a terminal disease. You're like, "But wait. How? When? Why? Oh, my goodness." It is complete. She lost. It was complete.

I went into real depression for several days. Then I thought, "Wow, I felt I lived through a really horrible presidency for eight years, being the Bush Junior's administration, [Vice] President Cheney." And it was devastating to me too because I am a news junkie. So, every day I watch the news. I was upset every day for eight years. But then we get Obama. It is going to be okay.

And it was getting better and better, and better, and better, and better, and better. And then we got Trump and the better lasted. He took credit for it. Okay. Who cares? Obama signified he does not care. That is fine. But Trump is riding that wave that Obama put him on. And COVID-19.

Blacklisting

I do not have feelings about it. I find it silly. When something is not worth the time to address, I do not address it. That is not worth the time to address. That is just silliness. That is just people acting like Donald Trump, with braggadocio. They are being bullies. I do not respond to that.

De Niro Feels the Urgency

Robert De Niro is one of the classiest, most dignified men in our business. And the fact that he feels propelled to speak out says how urgent it is.

It is urgent. We have a lunatic in the White House.

We have a really silly baby who got tall in the White House. And he is pretending to run the show. It's embarrassing because everybody's going, "What's going on you guys? This guy's a fool." We know, but we are having trouble dealing with him. Since he has the Senate, he can act like a tough guy. It is so unfortunate.

I just feel—to go back to what we started—Robert De Niro is going to speak out like that. He is moved to do so. If he is moved to do so, I move to listen and I move to get on board with that attitude, because we have pretty much the same politics. Trump has whatever politics are going to work for him that month. That is how Trump is. That is how he has always been. And he is just a weirdo with a big ego. That is all Trump is, a lot of money that his father made.

Is He Racist? He Speaks for Himself . . .

I do not want to call names, but I think he speaks for himself. He speaks for himself. And I think anybody who talks about people in categories has a racist tendency, anyway. That is because people are peeps, and women are women and men are men, and kids are kids. There is no difference. It is just what we are. So, yeah. He speaks for himself. I do not have to call him names.

Rallies and Trump's Ego

I do not have an answer for that. What is strange about Donald Trump is he is the opposite of everything the people who voted for him thinks he is. They think he is their buddy. They think he understands them because he is irreverent. So, he is one of us. He understands a bad system. He is one of us. That is what they are thinking he is. That is not what he is. What do they call them, those conventions that he gives, his little conventions?

Rallies. For instance, at those rallies, it is just for his ego and to feel insulated and agreed with. It is for his ego, those things. They do not get anything done. It is sad that it is allowed, but it has to be allowed. This is America. And the great thing for that being allowed is he exposes himself as a complete counterfeit, embarrassing ass that he is. Go Robert De Niro. Go.

Because He Chose Sides . . .

He chose sides. He was always on everybody's side. He was always anything he had to be. And then he became a Republican president. He had a side. He had a place. He had a job to do for the Republican Party, which is why I have an issue with the Republican Party. I think the Democratic Party helps America and the Republican Party helps the Republican Party. But I think that was the cut-off. He chose sides. He became a president.

Ronald Reagan? Let us be honest about Ronald Reagan, and nobody is . . . Ronald Reagan, [singlehandedly] in his terms in office, tripled the national debt. Think about that, tripling the national debt. Not doubling. Tripling the national debt. Oh my God, and we were in trouble, anyway. Because of Ronald Reagan, we will never recover from debt ever, because of that administration. And that is not an opinion. That is a matter of fact.

That being said, we have to start there and then go every other thing they say he did or didn't do, and take it apart because he was the worst president of the twentieth century up until Bush Jr. Then he was replaced by Trump being the worst. They have all been Republicans, and they have all been kind of used to be put in the office by the party, because they were usable.

They are all not terribly strong men, politically. They might be strong privately. I do not know any of them. Politically, Bush Jr., Ronald Reagan, and Donald Trump are not strong politically. They are bullshit artists, all three of them. One of them was a great speaker. Ronald Reagan could talk. Yeah.

I Turned Him Down Four Times . . .

I still insisted that Hollywood's hatred for Trump is personal, not because he chose the Republican side. It is way deeper. So, I asked Eric if he met Trump.

Eric: Yes, several times. I am the only guy I know who turned down his show four times, *The Apprentice*. And I said to my wife when he became president, I said, "Do you think he'll remember?" And she said, "Yep, you won't be invited to the White House." Okay. But I was never a fan.

I thought he was entertaining. I thought he had more humor about himself. He does not have humor about himself. I thought he did. I thought he knew he was kind of ridiculous, that he is kind of playing that. But he is not playing that. He kind of believes it, which I find disappointing because I was never a fan, but I was entertained by him to the nth degree. I love watching him speak because he was such a BS artist, and he was so much fun to watch him do that."

Daphne: Unlike previous inaugurations, Donald Trump's lacked any Hollywood or music A- Listers.

I told Eric how Andrea Bocelli had to withdraw from the inauguration, after he got threats.

Eric: Wow! I am horrified for him. That is horrible. But when that happens, wow, what would I do if that were me? I do not know. I do not know. It is horrible.

If I was invited?

No, I would not accept. Because we do not have a president. We have a guy living there, but we do not have a president. And our vice president is also spooky. Just think of anything happening to Trump and it was Pence, that is also spooky, but that is an opinion. So, that is what that is. Trump, he gives us every day enough facts to not wanting . . . as president, no matter what walk of life you are in, he is just horrible to this country.

It is not about him, being a reality TV star. No.

Had you asked me that eight years ago, I would have said yeah, but you are asking me now. Everything is reality TV. There is not a difference now between art and reality TV. It is all the same entertainment.

So, no, I do not think that is why. I think it is him. I think he makes his own bed every day of embarrassment.

Liberalism and Leadership

Hollywood—we both agreed—is mostly liberal.

Eric: Well, there is a very liberal walk of life, and art always has been, art always will be. And you will have your conservatives in every walk of life, but the West Coast in Hollywood is relaxed though for the most part. Back to Trump, if you are a leader, you must be a person worthy of followers. You must not fear the truth and must be committed to protecting people, almost mothering. And I do not see any of those attributes in Trump, not one.

I am not a leader. I am a hell of a follower. I am not a leader and know that I am not smart enough, and I am not kind enough. But I know that about myself. I regret it, but I know it. And he likes himself every day. He thinks he is a leader. He thinks he is it. It is sad.

Campaigning for Biden!

I am going to campaign for Biden. I am not going to be negative. Even this interview, what I did not want to have happened was trash Trump, trash Trump, trash Trump, because Trump is whatever he is. You have your opinions, and that is fine. And I have mine and they are mostly negative opinions, and they are mostly disappointment. But that is me. He speaks for himself and I allowed him to, because I do not have to say what he is or is not. Every morning when he gets those, what do they call them?

When he gets those press conferences that are not supposed to be press conferences. What is it supposed to be? It is supposed to be something else. But he uses that time to talk about himself and how hard it is to do all this, all these great things I have done, and all these lies. And yes, here is another lie, and here is another lie, and here is another lie. Okay. See you later. And it is like, "Wow, he just did that."

And then you have the newscaster come on and say, "That was a lie. That was a lie. That was a lie. That was a lie." And you go, "Yeah, I thought so too. Wow, that's mind blowing. This is our president." This is the guy. This is our guy. This is the guy who represents what we are, what we do, what we believe. And it is Donald J. Trump. Go Robert De Niro. Go.

Who Could Play Donald Trump?

I could not end this conversation without asking the actor who's always ready for the next role: Would he like to play Donald Trump? Eric: Wow. It is a great question. Who should play Donald Trump? I do not think we know him yet as a name. I think we have to find him. And I think he is findable. I think he will want to be found. Yeah. Because anybody who has got that physical type who can bluff the physicality, who has the innate core of loving a Donald Trump would really want to play that part. So, he is going to be findable.

Eric's bluntness would prepare him to face Donald Trump. So, I asked him: "If Donald Trump was sitting here instead of me, what would you say to him?"

Eric: Donald, the only thing I can do that can help you today is to tell you one thing. Stay away from microphones. Have all your peeps talk for you. It will make you more interesting. It will make you last longer, because you are going to bury yourself, buddy. Stay away from microphones. Do not get near them. You embarrass yourself every single morning.

The National Enquirer!

And then Eric wanted to add an interesting thought.

Eric: It is interesting to look at Trump's relationship to the *Enquirer*, with the owner. But I am bringing it up because of the *Enquirer* itself. That is a great magazine. Yeah, it prints a lot of trash, but it is always ahead of itself. In fact, I believe it was . . . Was it the O. J. Simpson trial? It was the O. J. Simpson trial that the *Enquirer* got so ahead of everybody else that you read stuff in the *Enquirer* the week before you had read it in the *Times*, in the *New York Times*, the same information.

So, I started buying the *Enquirer*. I am an *Enquirer* reader. I read the *Enquirer*. I read about myself occasionally and be like, "What?" It is funny. But as far as politics and world news goes, it is ahead of everybody else.

And you see what happened during the election, the last election, suddenly, instead of the usual sex and stuff, stories, there was all kind of the fat Hillary and Hillary going to die, and it was becoming very political.

Yeah. Yeah. All the name-calling, all the nicknames.

Trump understands the petty need in all of us because he is the petty need personified in life. He is so petty, and he is so needy, and he is so incomplete, and he is so lost. And he is the president of the United States of America. Go Robert De Niro. Say those things. Right on.

Chapter Three

Scapegoats

Scapegoats for divided America had also split right down the middle. There were two rigid categories. The conservatives were talking about "discrimination." The liberals were focused on "racism."

Lorenzo Lamas, as well as Kevin and Sam Sorbo made clear-cut cases on discrimination. They explained how they took the high road and left Hollywood, realizing there was no chance to make it there anymore because of outright discrimination against conservatives.

While Lorenzo left Hollywood altogether and became a pilot and never looked back, Kevin and Sam continued to make movies. They said, "Thank God for the independent movies!"

On the other hand, the life experiences of Too Short, Money B, and Eric B were perfect examples for racism in America. Glen "Big Baby" Davis, as a well-known and liked professional basketball player for the Boston Celtics and two other teams, had a varied experience compared to the rappers.

While rappers were pouring pains and sufferings into lyrics, Big Baby was coping with the norms of NBA, maintaining composure.

Discrimination

Lorenzo had enough with discrimination. By 2016, he had already left the entertainment industry and moved to the transportation business.

Kevin and Sam were realistic, like Lorenzo. They had also long moved from Hollywood to independent films.

It was clear to them, there was discrimination in Hollywood against conservatives, even worse against Trump loyalists.

Lorenzo Lamas

I'd tell Robert De Niro that I thought his performance in *Raging Bull* was one of the best performances I have ever seen and that is it.

I would not engage him in any political conversation.

—Lorenzo Lamas

Anything Lorenzo would add would be considered No-No rhetoric, come to think of it!

When Lorenzo Lamas told me he could not film with us for another week because "I am working," I was thrilled. Yes! At last, I found a pro-Trump supporter in Hollywood, who IS working. And in the middle of a pandemic.

Yay. . . Well. . .

A week later, a handsome Lorenzo joined Bill and I for lunch, before we filmed. The actor who is best known for his role of Lance Cumson, the irresponsible grandson of Angela Channing—played by Jane Wyman—in the primetime soap opera *Falcon Crest*, was realistic, and comfortable with his choices.

No, he was not working as an actor anymore. Realizing that the roles were long gone, he became a pilot, and the pandemic made him even more in demand.

Lorenzo did not put all blame on his political affiliation. He had another explanation, "Which is maybe relevant for Kevin [Sorbo] as well?" he suggested.

Actors who became known for their roles in long and successful TV series had become too identified with that one character, he suggested.

Maybe? Maybe not?

Looking at Hollywood from the sky above suits him well.

An Essential Worker: Pilot

Lorenzo Lamas: Well, fortunately I have been doing fairly well. I am a helicopter pilot. A full-time charter pilot for a company in Los Angeles, and we are an essential service because we do medical flights. We fly teams of doctors with the organs and we go all over Southern California dropping off the doctor's team and the organ to the different hospitals. So, we are a fully functioning helicopter company. So, I am extremely fortunate to be able to work as a pilot during this period of time. A lot of people are hurting and so, I count my blessings.

It is really tough for many now, what is going on now, than on ACRA strike or writer strike or an industry shut down for anything other than this. I recall a time when there was a six-month writer strike. This was in 1988, I think. And it did devastating damage to not only the actors and actresses that were working and producers and writers of course, but the crew. And many people that work doing the cameras and the lighting and the wardrobe and the continuity, all those craftsmen were forced to basically sell their homes, take their kids out of school that they were enrolled in that were not public. It was a devastating blow to the industry, and that was just six months. So, what is happening now because of the pandemic, is . . . Yeah, we will wait.

What is happening now with the pandemic is just gutting the industry . . . And I have talked to my agent three or four weeks ago. He said he does not have one client on a set anywhere. So, this is the worst of all possibilities because, why? Well, because not only is there no production other than yours and a few others maybe.

But there is no end. There's no . . . where does it stop? Where do we get back to work? When can we get back to work? That is the big question. So yeah, it's just been a devastating blow to the industry.

The Last Celebrity Apprentice

Lorenzo became part of history: He was cast in the 2014 *Celebrity Apprentice*. It would be the last show, because its host and exec-utive producer Donald Trump would announce he was running for president in 2015.

Lorenzo: I did *Celebrity Apprentice* with President Trump during the last season that he was able to do. That was 2014. We taped in 2014. It aired, I think, around 2015. And of course, then he announced his candidacy. So, I was in the last season and it was a wonderful experience to be able to do that.

Of all the reality shows that I have ever done before, *Celebrity Apprentice* was the one I wanted to do the most. And I had a very dear friend, a manager, and he was able to get me on the show because he had an exceptionally good relationship with one of the show runners for not only NBC reality programming, but also on the *Celebrity Apprentice*. He was able to get Dee Snider, the singer from Twisted Sister, my manager Ron Starrantino was able to get Dee, who is also a client of his, on the show.

So, one thing led to another and as I understand it my name was brought up in one of the executive board meetings and Mr. Trump was there and he said oh yeah Lamas, Lamas, he has a mother, Arlene Dahl. Wow. She was gorgeous. So, I guess I was in, thanks to my mom I was able to do that last season of that show. But I was able to do so much that I had not been able to do in film in a long time on *Celebrity Apprentice*.

I directed two commercials, I was able to also direct a photo shoot with [major league baseball player] Johnny Damon and his beautiful wife, Michelle Damon. It was a wonderful experience. Now, I got fired. I mean most people get fired. He sat across the table from me. He looked me right in the eye and goes, "Well Lorenzo, I'm sorry. You're fired." But it was such a great expe-rience because I got to do so many creative things on the show.

Donald, Melania, Eric, Lara Coming to the Bar

His most personal interaction with Donald Trump was after he was fired from the reality show and was sent home.

Lorenzo: After I got fired. You know, once a celebrity is given the boot, they usually go downstairs to the bar at Trump Tower, and relax for an hour or so and then they do the limousine scene, where the celebrity gets in the limousine with cameras and you talk about your experience and if you would have done anything differently and all that stuff. They get your take on being fired, right?

So, I am sitting at the bar and not really expecting anything except maybe to do the limo scene in whatever amount of time. And Melania comes down with Eric and his beautiful wife, and Mr. Trump. They come down to the bar to say goodbye to me. And I was told that that almost never happens. Like, you are a celebrity, you go to the bar, and then you get in the limo and you are back to the hotel and it was done. So, they came down with Melania and they told me that they really enjoyed how I represented myself on the show.

My charity, The Boot Campaign, is a charity that really helps the families of those that are deployed. So, if you have a loved one that is deployed, they are serving our country in the armed forces, and you have a problem at home, whatever that is, you are late on your mortgage or your car breaks down, or you have some issues with childcare, The Boot Campaign will step in and help whoever is left at home to take care of the family.

And so, I represented them, and because I represented such a noble charity, I have felt at the time during my last task that I was responsible. And I would not throw anyone under the bus on my team.

And so, Mr. Trump, Melania, and Eric, they said that they thought that was so honorable that they wanted to really thank me for stepping up and falling on the sword so to speak. So that meant a lot to me and it showed me that this is the guy that is obviously in a great position of power, and he is a tremendous businessman, phenomenally successful. And yet, he took the time to come down and thank a person that did the show. He didn't have to do that, and I'll never forget that.

I Was Surprised About Response . . . "His" Comments About Mexicans . . .

I did not feel like I knew him well enough to reach out to him, but I was friendly with Eric Trump. So, I did message Eric and I congratulated him, and I wished him and his family all the best. You know, I have always felt that the presidency of the United States has to be filled with an individual that understands how business runs. Because the United States of America is a business. We have multinational business interests. Multi-international business interests.

I always felt that a really good president would have the knowledge and the experience to be able to negotiate with foreign countries and to be able to negotiate from a position of strength. I mean, we are the strongest country in the world, financially, scientifically, culturally, and I always felt that it would take a leader with business acumen to really understand the office they hold. And to be able to put forth his ideals, his goals, and getting us back in the game and get us back in the universal game and put us up on top again.

The backlash after his remarks about Mexicans? I was surprised. I was surprised in the amount of vitriol that he received for comments that were taken totally out of context. I mean, if you go back and you look at that speech that he made establishing his candidacy and that Mexico is sending us their worst . . . That was a comment, look. He is not a politician. He is a man with a passion for this country. He is the most patriotic president bar none of anyone I have ever felt held that office. He loves this country.

What he was upset about was the fact that we were not doing anything to stem the flow of people that were coming in this country with mal-intent and bringing drugs and kidnapping children and bringing them into this country to be used as pawns in a very nasty and horrendous marketplace called sex trafficking.

This is a guy who had a passion and was not able to perhaps verbally make it politically correct, but I knew what he was saying. He was not calling Mexicans rapists and murderers and drug dealers. He loves people. I saw how much he loves people. All people. Because I was there in the board room and everyone was represented in the board room over the years of *Celebrity Apprentice.*

He never once singled somebody out because they were a woman or because they were of color or because they had a different political view than perhaps he did. Never once. If you watch all the episodes of *Celebrity Apprentice*, you show me one example of him being a racist or being a misogynist. Show me one example and I will give you it, but there is none, because he is not. But his statement was so skewed and so misrepresented by the media. That is what shocked me. I said, holy crap. They are going to try to destroy this guy.

And why? Because he is not a politician? Why? Because he is saying it like it is, he is telling us what we all know to be the truth? Why are they doing this to that man? And from that moment on I knew there was going to be a war that he was going to have to fight. But I also knew that if anybody could get in the fight, and to win it, it was going to be Mr. Trump. Because he is a winner.

The guys a winner. Say what you want to about his bankruptcies, I mean everybody, I have declared bankruptcy. Everybody does it because it gives us a fresh start. A new chance. You do not do it to hurt people, you do it so you can survive to invest again, to build another business, you know? To create another platform for people to be hired in to work. Do you know how many people he is hired, this man, in his private business? Do you know how many people?

You know his son Eric and Ivanka and Don Jr. Do you know how many people they hire in their businesses? Thousands of people they have hired, you know. I get in passion because I feel it is not fair, you know. The way that they are targeting this man. He gave up an extremely comfortable lifestyle, right? Comfortable, extremely comfortable.

Why? Because he believes in America, and he believes in this country, and believes in all the good that this country is capable of. He just wants to focus America on what is important, right? Freedom of religion, freedom to work, freedom for all individuals, black, white, Chicano, Asian, everybody. And he wants to give us all a chance and he wants to represent us in the world as the country that we should be represented as.

Trump Supporters Losing Jobs in Hollywood

My feeling about being ostracized for perhaps my political beliefs, it's hard for me to really pin it down. I mean I cannot really say that yes, I have been blackballed from Hollywood. A, because I have been a professional pilot from before Trump because president. I really have not made much of a political, I do not do a lot of political stuff on my social media. Every once in a while, I do, but I really do not generally speak.

So, I cannot say, but I think it is awfully strange how we do not see a lot of people in movies and television shows and so forth that have a public conservative image. I have some dear friends that are conservatives that I have not really seen a lot of out there in projects. So, do I believe there is a slight tendency to maybe shut out people of conservative values? Perhaps. I think there is more evidence that they would be shut out than that they would not be shut out.

It is pretty scary to have to think that your career could be ruined just for your beliefs in a political stance. We used to be able to disagree with each other. There was a time not too long ago where you would have a discussion with somebody who did not share your point of view, but it would be a healthy discussion. And you would understand their point of view. They would go out of their way to try to help you to understand their point of view. Now it seems like there is a lack of compassion and a lack of trying to understand the other person's point of view. There is such division now.

Such a Wide Division

I can never recall a division as wide as the one we are experiencing now between the liberal policies and the conservative policies. And I think the divide has widened because the policies have widened. I mean, the Democratic Party is not the same party as it was when I was young and first able to vote, right?

That was the Clinton party, that was the John F. Kennedy party, that was the Lyndon B. Johnson party, that was a party that had perhaps a different point of view. They were bigger government, more welfare programs for people that were struggling, and all of that I thought was fairly noble, as long as it did not infringe on my rights.

Because I have always been a pro-rights person. Everybody is right. Everybody has a right to their lifestyle. Everybody has a right to work where they want to work, to go to church where their faith takes them. And I did not like any government interference in that. And the Democratic Party was supportive of that for many, many years. It was just bigger government.

I am kind of a small government guy. I have always been that way, and I've always voted for the person, not the party. So, whoever is going to give me a platform of less taxes, more freedom, less infringement on my lifestyle, I am going to vote for them.

And in the last twenty years, it has been mostly Republican because they tend to be a little less government than the Democrats, but now, the difference is so vast and so wide. Now the Democratic Party is about so much more control over your life, you know. Not only more taxes but, my God, they want to be able to tell you that you cannot go to church right now.

You cannot follow your faith, what the hell is that all about? Wait a second? So, you are saying that we can go sit down in a restaurant now, take our mask off, and have a meal, with alcohol, but we cannot go to our favorite bar and sit down and have a drink? Or we cannot go to church on Sunday? That to me does not make sense.

How can we allow a person to go to a mass protest with thousands and thousands of people yelling at the top of their lungs, many of them not wearing any facial covering, but you do not allow people to go to church? That is a scary thought to me. And that's what's really disturbing a lot of people because there doesn't seem to be any consistency in this kind of movement to basically stop our freedom.

Racist? No Way!

Absolutely not. No way. I told you I do not think that that man has a racist bone in his body. I mean he has signed into law policies that help minority individuals. I mean, just one. . .

I witnessed it on *Celebrity Apprentice* . . . There was not anything racist at all, what I saw on the show. And as far as I know, not one person that ever worked on that show from the technicians to . . . they have never said anything about Mr. Trump being a racist. I think that is a drummed up, inflammatory accusation to also help to divide people in our country.

Hollywood Today, Preferring Blacks, Women?

In a period when Hollywood is reeling from #MeToo revelations and responding to the racial uprising around the country, some are concerned it may lead to "reverse racism."

Lorenzo: I think that's racist. Reversed racism, right? The fact that if you speak out in public favorably about either a president or about the policies that he is doing you get ostracized by all the people on social media mega sphere. Like Tim Allen for example, right? They canceled the show over remarks that he made that were considered conservative. So, that is wrong. That is another form of racism in my mind. Yeah.

Two Americas: Can We Talk?

Yes! I believe we can still talk to each other, but we have to tune out the noise that we are hearing. People have to stop watching the news 24/7. They have got to get off these devices all day long, because what those do is distract us from the goodness that is in our hearts. And we see so many examples of people on both sides of the fence coming together for the sake of humankind. Just remember after the 9/11 attacks how we came together as one, a one America.

We can do it; we just have to tune out the noise and listen to our hearts and . . . but there is something more important that we have to do. We have to really pay attention to what is behind the noise. What is behind the noise is a huge force that is trying to distract us and trying to control us, if you will. And there's people that believe that wearing masks will stop the spread, and I did not believe that in the beginning, very much so. I think that we were overwhelming the hospitals and that it was important to get that under control. But at this point, and the data and science that I have been able to read, supports the idea that most of us despite wearing masks will have either had the disease already, or get the virus and our body will go through what it will go through, and it will be done.

Did Hollywood Really Like Trump?

I only think Hollywood liked him because he was making money for them. That is the only reason why I think they ever brought him in to the inner circle of Hollywood, because he probably donated to other candidates, he probably donated to democratic candidates, I do not know this for a fact, but I would assume that he did donate. He had money. And Hollywood is mostly Democratic. And then once he announced his candidacy for president as a Republican they are like, okay we are done with him.

Hollywood Thinking About Trump is Sick

I don't really think he cares about Hollywood. I do not think he cares what people think. But I will tell you he is a street fighter. He is a New Yorker. You attack him, he is going to punch back. That is what I think. I do not think he worries too much about what people think about him. I think he has a purpose, and he knows his purpose and that is to make this country the greatest in the world again. It is to reinvest in the people of this country to bring us back up to the top.

So, does he really care about what Hollywood thinks? Eh, I do not think so. But I find it very telling that all the people that are speaking out against him in Hollywood, they are all basically fluffing their own bed. They are all on the same fluffing each other up. It is a sick, kind of a sick thing to do. I mean, you mentioned a couple of actors, they are getting the highest acknowledgement for their acting ability. The highest level, right, and academy award. And they take that moment where they could have thanked people in their life for getting them to that position or to thank the writers or the directors for giving them the material to be able to perform their role, and instead they. . . I do not know.

I think it is just a very incestuous, sick kind of thing that they do, these Hollywood people. I am glad I am out of it. I will be honest with you. I had a good run there, thirty years. Many television series, a few movies. I want to do that again. I don't know, I'm glad I got out of Hollywood because I think that it's a vastly different climate now.

"De Niro: I Would Defend My President Against Him . . . ."

I'd tell Robert De Niro that I thought his performance in *Raging Bull* was one of the best performances I've ever seen and that's it. I would not engage him in any political conversation.

I will tell you what I would do if given the opportunity or if I was put in the position. If Robert De Niro, if I overheard him bash our president, I would get in his face about it. I would absolutely, totally, get in his face.

I would defend my president against him because the attacks that I've sort of been made aware of that he has made . . . like, what is he trying to say? I mean, I just do not get it. I do not get why.

I do not know if I would try to talk with him . . . I have a problem with talking to people if I do not feel like they are open to a dialogue. I do not feel that people that are so filled with hate are open to really seeing another point of view. So, life is short. I'm not going to waste my time.

The American Dream: My Father

My father, Fernando Lamas, also was an actor and later on in his life was an exceptionally good director. Very much in demand for television. He was the most patriotic person that I have ever known. My father would put a flag out of his house if there was a Ralph's supermarket opening down the street. He loved this country. And he loved it so much because he aspired to be here.

When he was a young man in Argentina growing up, his dream was to make it in Hollywood. His dream was. . . he was a successful actor in Argentina before he was scouted to come up here under contract with MGM, so he finally made it and he was so proud of being an American. And he did it the right way, you know?

He applied for citizenship, he took an oath as a new American citizen, and I think it was one of his highest accomplishments of anything he had ever done in his life, was to become an American citizen. And that is the story of a successful immigration into this country. And I do believe that in my heart that he would be 100 percent behind our president as an immigrant.

That's all."

Kevin and Sam Sorbo

Did Kevin and Sam worry about Hollywood?

While Kevin was direct and realistic, Sam was her usual self all throughout their encounter with the filmmakers.

Her business was to poke at everyone that was not conservative, but she loved the Chinese the most, or so it seemed.

> Understatement of the Century: Hollywood used to like Donald Trump.
>
> —Kevin Sorbo

> Go hug a Chinese person.
>
> —Sam Sorbo

They were husband and wife performers—rather, he was the Hercules while she was a princess. The filmmakers viewed them as they presented themselves. Anyone who recognized them in the hotel lobby was also doing the same.

They were working hard to produce. They were not complaining or blaming others. The facts were facts. There was no reason to deny them. Independent movies were it for them. There was not much else to do in Hollywood.

They had come to Palm Beach, Florida, for the documentary filming. They were saying that they were there to look for a new home. The fact that they were finally migrating to Florida, a conservative state and not one known as a hub for prominent film making, was saying a lot to these filmmakers.

As Trump loyalists—rather, as conservatives—it was no secret that Florida was a destination like Texas or Nevada had become in America.

***

The meeting place for the shoot was the Brazilian Court hotel in Palm Beach. It was pouring rain that day, yet no weather was going to prevent these filmmakers from delaying the project.

The cameraman was local, a pro they had worked with previously, so they trusted him.

In California, their crew was a husband-and-wife team. They were like a family to them and they were careful about their exposure.

So, their requirements in Florida, Washington, DC, and New York had to be the same: a crew they knew.

***

Other complications were not an excuse either to delay or postpone anything, even their stolen car.

Relocating Back to Palm Beach: Spending More Time with President Trump

Kevin and Sam Sorbo were just relocating from Tampa to Palm Beach when we scheduled the filming. He is an avid golfer, and what could be a more perfect location than this area? Naturally, as a supporter of Donald Trump, he was checking out Trump's clubs at the area as well. Sam is an actress as well. She is most known as Serena on the television series *Hercules: The Legendary Journeys,* in which Kevin starred.

Bill and I arrived in Palm Beach in the middle of the radical uprising and looting after the death of George Floyd. The city was under curfew after 9:00 p.m. The jewelry and high fashion shops were boarded up with wood. We arrived late at night. The streets were dark, empty, scary. A few hours after our arrival, we discovered that our rental car was stolen. The police told us it was not the only car theft that night.

The next morning, we met the Sorbos. They are a team: They act together, write and produce together, and complete each other's sentences. They are both tall and good looking.

Right after we met, I called our friend Robin Bernstein, the US Ambassador to the Dominican Republic. She was isolating in

Palm Beach and was about to join us with her husband Richard for lunch with the Sorbos.

"Sam Sorbo is stunning!" I warned Robin. "Glam up for lunch!"

Over lunch in a popular local spot, Kevin told us how he lost the role of Superman to Dean Cain.

"But I got to play Hercules for several seasons! When I go to Greece, I get so many cheers."

Unlike the Bernsteins and us, who have seen Trump regularly, Kevin and Sam have not. Kevin had met Trump once, a long time ago.

They are both vocal Trump supporters. Sam looked serious when she told us, "When Kevin told me he was thinking of going out and supporting Trump, I told him: 'Well, you should prepare yourself . . . We should prepare ourselves to give up on some jobs.'"

Sam had an interesting theory about why Hollywood hates Trump. "He is the most pro-life president. He is very pro freedom. But I think the reason that they really hate him is because of China. Yeah. You do not see that coming. Well, China is communism, and they love communism. They love it. He ran on setting things straight with China and they joked about it and were like, that is not going to happen. Remember when he finally banned the flights from China, they were like, 'What? How dare he. That is an awful thing to do. He is such a xenophobe.' No, we love China. Go hug a Chinese person."

She continued: "Disney is in bed with China and the other studios are in bed with China."

Kevin was as firm in his beliefs.

Palm Beach: Facing Violence and Curfew

Kevin Sorbo: Well, it's incredibly sad to see what's going on because they've gone past now the assault on this poor man who was killed by bad cops, and there are bad cops. Let us face that.

But most police officers are wonderful people, and it is very sad to see the response because now it has nothing to do with, it has to do with, from what I am hearing, paid groups of assaults going on all over [big cities across the nation].

Recent Looting

React to this by looting? By destroying public and private property? This is crazy, and this is the same stuff that went under in Ferguson [Missouri] and Baltimore years ago. Now it is happening again, but it is even worse this time around because we are not doing anything to stop it. We are getting these governors and these mayors who are not doing things to stop these horrific assaults on their town and on the people that live in these cities.

Probably China is laughing all the way to the bank, right? I mean, scary.

I have got a lot of friends in Europe, and they are all saying the same thing, how sad and ridiculous it is. It is even, I saw something going on in Vancouver, Canada, now as well, where they were attacking police officers. They were all dressed up in the riot gear there as well. So, there is a lot of anger out there, and a lot of it came from what was going on with the COVID right now, because they have forced us to stay away from everybody. Now it is proving to be as harmful as a bad flu season. Yet they are still making people, do not do this, do not do that. But now, if you notice all the rioters, they are not practicing any social distance, are they?

So, I guess it is okay if you are rioting and looting and destroying people's businesses. Their thinking: "Right, we deserve this television set. It is mine."

Oh, I saw women running out with cheesecakes too. Must be graduation cheesecakes, I do not know.

Political Involvement

Sam told us, "When I first met Kevin, I discovered that he was conservative and that was one of the reasons that we fell in love, because we have similar worldview and I like him. Conservatism is basically a Judeo-Christian worldview. Okay. Where we believe in freedom. We believe in the sovereignty of the individual."

Kevin: "I have, but it wasn't until about ten years ago when I noticed if you were vocal about being in your politics, that didn't go with the majority of Hollywood, the liberal crowd, then there was more of a backlash. I did not notice that back in the nineties and even in the beginning of 2000. But you get in 2008, 2010, it really became an issue with people. It is too bad because I believe that we should all have a voice. Hollywood started out as a very conservative place. Jack Warner, all these guys that formed these studios, they were conservatives. But the sixties really changed things in America. The whole hippie movement, the free love movement, the whole abortion issue in the early seventies was reaching a peak. Then you had obviously the Vietnam War.

I Voted for Ronald Reagan

The first time I could vote, I voted for Ron Reagan in 1980, and I grew up in Minnesota, and my parents are Hubert Humphrey, Walter Mondale. I know. You know what is interesting about Minnesota, I mean, through the years now, it is turning into more of what California politics are. It is unbelievable to me. Because if I look at Hubert Humphrey today, even if you look at JFK. I always tell my liberal friends, look at John F. Kennedy's inauguration speech in 1960, and tell me if there is one Democrat that talks like that today. There is not. What is on his gravesite? Ask not what your country can do for you, but what you can do for your country. There is not a Democrat that believes in that today. They say, "We'll take care of you from cradle to grave.

We will take care of you. Don't worry about it." It is control, it is power.

Reagan, I believe, I could be wrong, but I am pretty sure he was a Democrat at one time.

Trump was the same. Then he said "I didn't leave the party. The party left me." I know a lot of people in history that have said that same thing. I think Jon Voight even said it that way. That I think he believed at one time, I mean, he looked at more social issues he believed in and fought for. But in the end, he saw, he said, "Wow, it's just getting too crazy." I think both parties are moving more and more and more to the left, which is unfortunate. The whole country is. I do not know. Before President Trump ran for office, he was loved by Hollywood. As far as I could see.

Understatement of the Century: Hollywood Used to Like Trump

He was loved by Hollywood. I mean, they had him on all the shows. They loved them. The minute he jumped over to the conservative side and said, "Enough is enough with what we're doing to this country," and obviously tens of millions agree with him. Then they started hating him.

If Trump is a Racist, so is . . .Lincoln

Sam Sorbo did not need any time to think about it. While violent threats took over the streets around us, including the "Winter White House," Mar-a-Lago next door, she said: "In light of the protests? No. I think if Trump were a racist, he is an insult to racists everywhere . . . I think what he has done for minorities has been remarkable. So, if he is a racist, he is like the worst example of a racist, you know what I mean? It is like, sure Lincoln was a racist too then, why not? I mean, the other thing is it has become almost meaningless. Sadly."

Kevin: They throw out the race issue right away. I said, "Just show me an example where he's a racist," and no one can say it.

It is just labelling they like to throw at people. "You're a racist." Then they just keep it at that. They do not give any reasons why.

I do not have any proof for it. He [Trump] has done more for the African American community than any president's done in decades. If they were honest about it, look, the unemployment records, just helping. He has been out there doing everything he said he was going to do. This virus is the only thing that has really exploded everything he has helped to create over the last three and a half years. It is unfortunate that this is going on right now, but to blame him for everything. . .

Look, he could say something that every liberal says behind closed doors, but because he says it, they will disagree with him in public. It does not matter. He is damned if he does, damned if he does not. So, it is a horrible situation to be in, and it is a thankless job. I would not want it. I am not qualified for it anyway, but I would not, it is crazy.

That is true. But God bless he is doing what he has been doing, but right now, think he's got to step in a little stronger with what's going on with these riots!

It was interesting during the debates to see when he was debating all the other candidates on the Republican side. I think when they got down to the last half a dozen or so people, I kind of went along with Ann Coulter. I saw her on the Bill Maher show, and they said, "Who do you think's going to win the presidency right now at this point?" She said, "Donald Trump," and they all laughed at her. I was like going, "I don't think she's that wrong." Obviously, she was right, completely right.

Racist and Fascist Trump

"He's a racist." Show me his racism. "He's a fascist." Man, I look at these Antifa guys, these punks that are out there running in the streets with their mask on.

Because everybody has got to wear a mask now, anyway, they are making us, and they say they are against fascism. Well, they are the fascists. Nazi stands for national socialism. These are the people that want socialism.

We are letting these people run the streets and ruin our country.

I do not know, I would just like them to tell me, without getting angry about it, without screaming. Everybody is just yelling at the top of their lungs.

I mean, I've seen De Niro just go off, and I'm going, "What is going on?

Give me the reasons why you have so much hate and anger for a guy that's actually made the country better. I'm sure behind closed doors, they've got admit even to themselves. "Yeah, he's done a pretty good job." But they, for whatever reason, it is just the rage feeds on itself. It is just, you see it with the riots. I think there is a lot of people out there doing these things and looting. I think when they get back to their homes, I hope they have soul, conscience, and they going, "Why did I do this? I shouldn't have done this." But they get caught up in it all.

His Rhetoric: Bullying is Too Much

It was the first time Kevin Sorbo paused. The first time, he admitted he had a doubt (though temporary) about Donald Trump. I asked about Trump's blunt—sometimes bullying—rhetoric.

Kevin: Like a lot of people, I think I was turned off with some of the way he treated some of the other candidates on stage. I thought there was no reason to be that way. But to me, it is only 10 percent of the things he said. The other 90 percent of the things he was saying, even in his tweets, I find them humorous. Everybody takes everything so serious. I will post things all the time on Twitter and Facebook. When I post the truth, I post facts, I get attacked left and right. People do not want to hear the truth. They want to be lied to. They enjoy being lied to, apparently. All I do is put facts out there. So, I started looking at things he is doing. It is really the only outlet he has because the media is not going to ever give them a fair shake.

I have never seen a president, there has never been a president, that every single day gets attacked the way he gets attacked. Right now, they just want him out. They want to see America fail. They are enjoying seeing the riots. That is why they are not doing anything about it, because it is really the blue states. By the way, do you know that the conservative states used to be the blue states? I do not know when that switched. I believe it was right after Reagan. Because I do not think—this is my hypothesis—they did not want to be associated with the color red, of communism. Because when you look at the map, when Reagan won 49 out of 50 states against Mondale from my home state of Minnesota, which Mondale barely won Minnesota, I think by four points, it was blue states. Then I do not know, they switched it.

It is like separation of church and state. When Jefferson put that in there, it is not in the constitution. It was put in to keep government out of churches. They have switched it around. They said, "No, you can't have anything to do with any, in the schools or anything that has anything to do with God." We took God out of the schools in 1964, took the Bibles out. We give them to prisoners. So, what does that say? But how has our school system been going over the last fifty, sixty years? It is incredibly sad what we are doing to America.

Well, I always had a little, where I am in the industry of Hollywood that screams for tolerance and freedom of speech. But it's completely a one-way street on both of those angles.

Hollywood? Thank God for Independent Movies!

Whether one is left- or right-wing, Kevin and Sam Sorbo would win people over with hard work, and their constant search for new projects. They do not sit and wait for offers . . . they like to create their own opportunities.

No need to throw pity parties for them.

Kevin: Hollywood owes me nothing. I have had a very great career. I had two wonderful series that I was a lead in. How many actors can say they had two series that went five years and seven years? Not many. I have shot over sixteen movies since then. Thank God for independent movies. Because if I did not have independent movies, I would not have a career anymore.

But to me, ultimately [it] just comes down to finding it incredibly sad that we cannot get past the ridiculousness of the politics of everything and just want to be in a business that I still love. I still love being on a movie set. I love the creative process. I love working with people on both sides of the camera. This business is probably more important to me now than it has ever been. I still want to keep making movies that have hope and faith and redemption and stories that are positive instead of all the negative stuff. Because Hollywood puts out a lot of anger, a lot of violence, a lot of hate. A lot of that is supported in a way to be passed on to generation to generation, and that's sad.

Dumped by Hollywood Agents
Well, sure. Look, I recently just signed with an agent again, after years.

ICM was my agent, and they said, "We got to part ways." My manager said, "I can't get you in."

It was interesting. She said, "Maybe you should run from office because you get so political." I started laughing, I'm going, "Every Hollywood actor that's an A-lister out there. We all knew who the A-listers are, are full-on liberals and full-on social-ists." I was saying, they are all very wealthy. They can afford to be socialists. So, they do not live that lifestyle, but they know what is right for everybody else, right? But yeah, it has made a difference certainly in the auditions I have gotten. Like I said, if it were not for independent movies, I would not have a career, so I am thanking God for independent movies,

ICM. . . yep, they made a lot of money off of me on two series.
It is okay. It is what it is. I do not hold grudges against them.
If that is the way they want to do business, that's fine.

Blacklisting

I laugh at that stuff because what it comes down to is the hypocrisy. It is not just on the left in Hollywood. It is the liberals everywhere. It is do as I say, but not as I do. The hypocrisy is so bla-
tant, constantly. Politicians of every level can say whatever the
heck they want to say right now. A day later they can say the
opposite. You can say, "Well, we have you saying right here that
the sky is blue." I said, "No, no, I meant the sky is red. I never
said that."

"Well, you're saying it right here." They can just deny it.
They do not care anymore. Lies mean nothing to politicians anymore. They can lie all the time. It is unfortunate. It's unfortunate, but it's the world we live in now and the world that people
are okay with, which makes it even more insane.

Lost Jobs . . .

I can't even begin to know what jobs I lost or what potential. I
mean, I see all this stuff coming out in cable and on networks.
There is a lot of jobs. I said, "Well, I would have been right for
that job. It would have been nice to audition for it." But I do not
get called in for that anymore. I do have a new agent now. I said,
"We'll see what happens." He is in Los Angeles, and I was very
straightforward with him. I said, "This is what's happened." He
is aware of it. But he sees how well I have done on my own. I had
worked very hard on my own to create my own production company and find my own funding. I have three new movies coming
out this year. Well, they won't come out this year because all the
theatres are closed.

I Met Trump Fifteen Years Ago

Kevin and Sam Sorbo handed their loud support to a man they did not know. They made a key decision which would impact their careers and personal lives, based on Trump's media appearances and promised policies.

Kevin: It was a long time since I met him. We saw each other up in Lake Tahoe. So, it has been a long time, about fifteen years ago. So, it has been a long time. We got to golf at that American Century Golf Tournament. We had a wonderful lunch together and we chatted. But at that time, we were talking about *The Apprentice*, because that was the hot show at that time.

He asked me a couple of questions about the business, and he said, "It's the number one show on TV, and they want me to do another season. Do I have to do another season?" He knew darn well that of course he must do it. Because even if he is only on it for five minutes at the end, people wait for him to go, "You're fired." That is what they wait for. Because it was a great show, and it ran a long time, and made a lot of money for NBC, I think it was.

Why Hollywood Hates Trump

Sure. Yeah. I think even the conservatives in Hollywood, I mean the conservatives in Washington, DC, were not fans of Reagan, and I think Donald Trump is getting that same backlash even from people within his own party because he is not one of them. We need term limits. I do not know why we cannot, as it is, we the people, right? So, I do not know why we cannot say no more fifty-year careers for you bozos. You get eight years max and you move out. If the president gets eight years, that is all you guys get.

Because the trouble is, they get so embedded in that world. I have always wondered. I put a thing out there on Twitter and Facebook saying, "Why are you so upset about a billionaire who becomes president? How do you become all multi-multi-millionaires working in the service of politics to better the world, better America when you are doing quite the opposite of it? So, yeah, I think you get six to eight years and you are done, move on. So, I do not know why we do not, as citizens of America, fight for term limits right now.

All I see is this anger and hatred and anything and everything that they can do to get Trump out of office. It goes back to your first question, your first theory, is he is not one of them.

He is a guy that bucked the system. He is a businessman. He is, what made America great, was not big government. What made America great were individuals. That is what this country was founded on and set up to be. So, because he does not kiss their ass and does not play the game with them, he is hated. He's hated and hated and hated.

De Niro

Oh my gosh. I do not want to tell him anything. I would like to know the seed that was planted in them. Because when I look at a De Niro just go crazy, a Rob Reiner, who I have total respect for as a director. I have met him before. I go, just give me the reasons why instead of just blanket. . .

Hollywood Hates Egos?

Sure [Trump] was. No question he was part of Hollywood.
I do not get it. That is why I want them to tell me. Is it because he started promoting things that even JFK promoted? I get it, that people get upset with some of the tweets he puts out there. I love it when they tell me, "He's got such a big ego," and I go, "Obama didn't have an ego? Any president we've ever had in America, doesn't have an ego?" Give me a break.

You need an ego to have a job like that. You got the most powerful position in the world. Of course, you must have an ego. So, I do not know. I do not know. I do not have an answer for that. I know you are looking for one from me, but I do not get it.

I would love to have them sit on this couch with us and explain to us in a rational voice instead of an angry one.

Golf Can Help Solve the World's Problems

If we played an association game, the name *Trump* will trigger *golf*. Trump had criticized Barack Obama for golfing. I recall that when I helped his son Eric Trump, promoting a charity at their Westchester Golf Club, Donald Trump (way before becoming a president) was careful to avoid being caught by my camera crews.

Yet, Trump's presidency would be connected optically to him golfing at his different clubs. Kevin Sorbo suggested a spin: "If it was Donald Trump there, I would say, "Mr. President, let us go golfing. We can talk about this on the golf course." That is what I would say to him.

We would solve all the world's problems on the golf course together. Obama golfed a lot. I love the fact that they are attacking Trump for golfing for the first time in three months. Obama golfed more than any other presidents ever golfed. Bush even stopped golfing after 9/11 happened. To me, I am going, 'I don't know, if I was president, I'd be golfing a lot too,' because the reality is you can get a lot of work done out there.

The actual time spent hitting a ball and playing the round of golf in a four-hour round of golf is maybe ten minutes long. Because I play quick. So, when anybody hits a golf ball, boom. Then you are walking 250 yards to your tee shot, you have plenty of time to talk to the press, talk and answer questions, take care of business. So, I think I would get a lot of work done on the golf course. Really."

Racism

Daphne posed the question to all twenty-four interviewees: "Is Trump racist?"

Most answered quickly. No one said outright that he is racist. Those defending Trump came up strong. Some were angered by the question but mostly they laughed at it and further ridiculed those who thought that Trump was racist.

African Americans preferred to give examples of racism but did not voice their opinions on calling the forty-fifth president racist. Rightly so, because they have never met Donald Trump in their lives. Two of them had clear opinions though. They both met Trump. They were split down the middle.

Eric B met Trump twenty years earlier and interacted with him extensively. He praised Trump for being frank and smart. Claudia Jordan, on the other hand, was the only one that came out to say that she now was thinking that Trump is racist.

Too Short and Money B provided chilling stories. For them, racism was not a scapegoat, it was a reflection of real fear and anxiety. Big Baby Davis did not show fear or anxiety, but he put his finger to the problem, literally and physically.

Too Short

A lighthearted comment from Too Short:

> But I just told you one thing that I would say, but I probably would just roll up a joint and pass it to Trump and say, "Chill, bro!"

Only because Daphne was smartly thinking if there was a way to bring the well-known rapper and the president on the same page.

During the filming, there was no reason or need to smoke a joint to chill because there was no tension in the bungalow of the Beverly Hills Hotel, even though both filmmakers were white and Trump delegates.

When Too Short mentioned, off camera, how life has changed in LA, he was talking about a harsh reality for himself and America.

Since the filmmakers had filmed with Mark Geragos few weeks earlier in downtown LA, what Too Short was saying was no surprise.

Ever since they met Too Short, they meant to visit him in his office but their reluctance to go to downtown LA eventually disappeared. Governor Gavin Newsom suddenly issued an ordinance that closed down everything in California.

As a result, they never made it to downtown LA again for the entire year of 2020. The reports about the city were so disturbing over time that even passing through the city by car became questionable.

Hysteria eventually started to become a bigger problem. That was the reality when they met Too Short for the interview, just days before the Beverly Hills Hotel shut its doors, ending life as they knew it for Hollywood.

I Have Millions of Followers

Todd Anthony Shaw, known by the stage name Too Short, came to meet with us at the set we built at the Beverly Hills hotel.

Too Short became famous in the West Coast hip hop scene in the eighties, with songs often based on pimping and drugs.

Yet, he has maintained his fan base religiously. It is his bread and butter, and he knows it.

***

Too Short: My one million Instagram followers or something, the millions of Too Short fans, my fan base is very, very, very, very, very various. I am from the San Francisco Bay area and it is out there as far as how we get along and live together.

And my fan base, all around, is a diverse age group and ethnic groups, as well as economic groups. And when we get together on music and you come to a Too Short concert, I could do a show in Malibu at a little bar club, something, a house party, and then go over to Watts and do another party the same night. And we are talking about people with completely different political views and social views.

***

While the pandemics forced him to cancel all his shows, he was recording an album with other rappers: Ice Cube, Snoop Dogg, and E-40.

He and Arshia Bolour, his manager, shared with us some of the behind the scenes of four mega rappers, four managing teams, handlers in between, collaborating.

He has a big studio downtown, where he is planning to do something for the youth when life gets back to normal.

While he looks reserved, he has been bearing so much pain. When he started to talk about his personal experience with day-to-day racism, it was hard to digest.

When he begged: "STOP IT!

He meant every letter of it—"it" meant—the hatred.

He was even receptive, during the interview, to explain to Trump how hurtful some of his rhetoric was.

And then, he decided, he would not.

Just Stop the Hating!

Too Short: Well, when you say 50/50 speaking on politics and you go to blue to red, the Democrats to Republicans, 50/50, I think 50/50 and the year of 2020 in America, we're thinking all of these things. We're like, "Are you a Democrat? Are you a Republican? Are you a racist? Are you not?" We pick out all these things like, "All the racists and Republicans over there. All the Democrats and liberals and the non-racists over there." And I do not think it is like that. I don't think we're that simple of a nation to just go, "Every Republican is racist. Every Democrat is a liberal. Every Democrat is liberal and not racist. And it's just split in two."

I think it is a whole bunch of us just in all groups. So, I think the conversation is just to say, "Not so much as who are you, but what are you going to do?" Because we can talk about who are you? How did we get here? What are the conditions now? What were they? All you really got to do is just stop. Just stop.

Daphne: When you first came into the scene, it was really in a way, like a protest. The way you protest. It was really a movement. And then, in my personal feeling, it was sort of going less on the front seat and the issue was less on the front seat. Now they are back. What do you do about it? Are you writing new music, or . . . ?

Too Short: Well, we definitely, even at my age, I still make music and what is happening in the community affects my music. It comes in the music. No doubt about it. So, when I am writing a song today in 2020, current events get mentioned and I am very opinionated about what is going on right now. And if these are not new opinions, based on the developments of 2020, I have been feeling this way since I was a child. I have been feeling this way since I was a young adult. I base these opinions on experiences and not personal experiences, not other people's experiences, not what I read or saw, but when I experienced. So, I have a lot to say in the conversation, but I think that every time it comes my way, I am going to say the same thing. If you want to fix this, you have to stop.

Stop the hating, stop the aggression. You were taught this. You were not. . . I am not speaking to you; I am just saying. You were taught the hate. If in any instance, if you put these little kids of different religions and different races and different social backgrounds, economic backgrounds, you put them in a room together, little kids, they will love each other and they will play. You have to teach them to hate each other. At some point you just got to stop. The conversation is [expletive] if you keep doing it over and over again from Jim Crow to civil rights to mass incarceration, to why, why, why it's inner city, and why? Just somebody at some point's got to stop.

Somebody with a Microphone Has Options!
Hollywood players endorsing political candidates have become louder since Donald Trump announced he was running.

Too Short: I think that regardless of what our personal opinions are about what you could do with the camera and media, it's going to happen anyway. If you think that somebody should, or should not, or how they should use it? Should their news use it only, should Hollywood media use it, should the music industry use it? I think it is just another tool that is available. If it was a really long time ago and the only way to spit out your propaganda, to spew out your propaganda was through pamphlets or something. You pass it out, pieces of paper.

That is no different than social media posts and you just passing out your opinion. And I think that media, for a long time, a long, long time, it is like God and in America. You could write a story in a paper long before television was out, and that story would change all these people's opinions. And it has not changed. You could send out, right now, just think of the craziest thing off your head and tweet it and then somebody reposts it and it is just whatever. And it becomes a thing. It could become a thing just through the way our media has grown.

So, to tell somebody who has access to an audience who has a camera, or has a microphone to keep your opinion to yourself is almost impossible. So, no matter how we feel about it, it is going to happen anyway. You got people who can really rush a stage and I do not have to give you any instances, any scenarios, because you know what happened. Somebody is on the platform and they are speaking what they believe. Somebody else ran to the stage, grabbed the mic, and yelled out just in time before security grabbed them. You know what I am saying?

That is the power of media. That moment probably will be more popular than the actual person who was there giving a speech or the presentation. So, I do not think we are in control of this monster, that I called the media. I do not know what you call it, and I am not talking about news people. The media is powerful, and it can print it, you can write it, you can tweet it, you can put it on a billboard. It affects somebody who sees it and absorbs it. And they base their opinions on whatever. And I think it all goes back to your own belief system, the things that you were taught and the things that you believe and then you absorb all these things that are coming in and you were to inter-pret it. I think that way down there, a lot of people were taught wrong things. A lot of people were given bad tools to work with.

Racism is Not New

It's not new anywhere you go. I also feel like in America we have these racist opinions about each other. They go from stereotypes to just ignorant in differences that we do not know the truth about. It is not white people hating black people. It is a lot of hate in between the communities. It is a lot of hate in between religions. It is a lot of hate and I do not see any other way around this. You can tell me all you want to tell me about how we can give things back right? But how are you going to get anywhere with all of the preconceived hate. You are hating me for some-thing your great grandfather told you to hate me for and maybe he was wrong. I do not know. But you are like, "I'm going on that. I hate you because you are brown."

People hurt and you see blood and it is always somewhere else. It is here now, and it has been here, but we do not want to know the truth. You do not want to know how many times I was in George Floyd's position and either was arrested with-out dying or arrested or just let go and the incident is not even documented. How many times I had a knee on my back while I am being handcuffed for suspicion. And then when you are no longer suspicious, it is like, "Oh, you're free to go." There is not even a ticket or anything to say that ever happened for your complaint to be valid.

It is not new. It is really not new. I think many, many, many years before the civil rights movement, people who were very respectable, people of color who were very respectable, had to think to themselves—especially black men—you had to think to yourself before you walk out your house and go to work every day, "I hope I don't run into a crazy white guy who's just mad for no reason because your life could get . . . It is so many ways that it is not new. All you have to do is say, "He did it." He could have been at home with his kids the night before. You say he did it he is going to be in jail for the rest of his life. And he can say he did something that did not even happen, and he is still in trouble. So, I think when you asked me about 2020, it is not about 2020. What is going on, this is not from right now. This is not from George Floyd.

Some of us have been walking around, getting knees on our neck, and others of us have been walking around and putting knees on necks. And the only words you want to say is stop. When a knee is on your neck, that is the only word you want to get out is, "Can you stop?" And when your knee is on somebody's neck, do you need to be telling yourself, if not your partner or somebody on the sidewalk, "Stop. He's dying."

***

Daphne: And Trump: Did he push racism further?

Too Short: I don't know Donald Trump. I have not been around him. I have seen people like Omarosa [Manigault Newman] speak on him. I have seen his cast on the show, *The Apprentice* show. It was not all white people. I do not know if Donald Trump hates black people or people that are not white. I do not know if he hates. What I do know that in order to hype up crowds he feeds things to the people that hate. So, he gives them something. But if you are in war, so to speak, Republicans against Democrats, you are fighting a war. So, I guess, like I said, one of his tools is hate!

Looking from my angle, part of my job is to stand in front of thousands of people and get them excited. And I know many ways to do it. I can do it without music. In between songs, I can say things and they could be about race or police or about a party. And I can get a reaction from the crowd, a cheer, or any kind of reaction. You have that ability. You can work a crowd while you are giving a lecture.

And Donald Trump is good at that. He is good. He is good. So, you cannot lie. We cannot sit here and tell lies to ourselves to say we did not see what he saw. How he plays around with words. He will not be our leader who stands in front of us and goes, "Everybody, let's get along." He will not say it.

Deep down, that is not a good strategy for him in this liberal-controlled media. A lot of people clearly, Barack Obama went through the same thing. The day you are elected, half the country goes, "I hate you." Every president of late has to go through that. I cannot remember, I do not even know in my lifetime, all the presidents I have seen be elected were half hated and half loved.

Sitting Down with the Opposition

Those are things that show you have the ability to humble yourself at times and when you are sitting down with the opposition, so to speak, a little humble behavior doesn't hurt. You know what I am saying? And that would be a great gesture. It would a great gesture. I do not have to be the truth, but it would be a great gesture.

Of course I would sit down with any grown man that wanted to sit down and have a conversation. And I would just say four years. If you get four more, just kind of, you do not have to do to the whole hate thing. You are in now. You have got your next four years. Just get to get the business because you do have an agenda and I know the agenda is not to make us hate each other.

***

Daphne: He would tell Trump to be more sensitive to words.

Too Short: I just feel like when it comes to advisors, I don't know. I am just assuming, but I assume that all presidents have a ton of advisors. All politicians at a higher-ranking level, politicians have a ton of advisors and these advisors are like shields. They are supposed to deflect and stop things that might get spun out of control in a negative way. It does not appear to be that there is a ball of advisors in front of Trump that just say, "All you got to do is not say that little phrase there, or don't use that word or don't refer to them as that." Those little things, it's literally, the words are sort of the black mark on this presidential track record so far."

It is a Comedy . . . Does He Know He is Funny?

Yeah. And you cannot sit there and just dissect every president we had. Like George Bush. We like to get the comedians and stuff, want to get to George Bush Jr. on his one-liners and make fun and try to play like he is a little frat boy. The personalities we give our presidents. Jimmy Carter with Southern accent and the peanuts. But Trump is, his are those statements. Those statements. Obama, we made a lot of fun of Obama. We made a lot of fun of Obama. He was walking in circles. He could not get things done. They made fun of the way he talks really slow and pauses in between, and it was just, everybody has their thing. And then

Trump, they just, the comedians are just like, it is spot on. And they just blurt out these things, these things that he tweets. And it is funny, it is comedy. Does he know it is funny? Does he?

What Words Would He Tell Trump Not to Use?

I think just show some sensitivity. In so many instances where we stop everything we are doing, we cut off every television program and we cut to breaking news or we cut to the leader, the commander-in-chief who is about to tell us something. And there is just a level of insensitivity that it hurts. It hurts when you watch it and you are waiting for just some compassion, just some glue. Stick us together. And you do not, you are not the glue. You will not be the glue. You will not be human; you will not be emotional.

You just run it down really fast and walk away from the podium. And it is like, "Don't you care?" That is what people say. "You care about this, but not that." You got to be the commander-in-chief. You have got to keep your people together. When you say, "I'm about to go kick somebody's ass" your army is all races. They come from all walks of life, not just your favorite group of people. The army's not all Republicans or all red states. It is all of us. So, keep us together. That is all. And a little compassionate sensitivity would go a long way. You do not need to be, and I know the thing is that it is that very condescending facial expression. And it is so arrogant.

And it is like on one end, I want my leader to have that face, like "Yeah, I'm that motherfucker," excuse my language. But on the other hand, I am like, "Damn, dude." It is a little spoiled brat's facial expression. And I am like, "Just smile. Something."

I Would Offer Trump a Joint

But I just told you one thing that I would say, but I probably would just roll up a joint and pass it to Trump and say, "Chill, bro."

Money B

Too Short suggested that we include rapper Ronald Brooks, known as Money B. They both grew up in Oakland. Money B showed up at our set with his father, a former Black Panther.

The two are very close, and when Money B talks about him, his eyes are sometimes tearful. They have a special father-son bond, despite a challenging beginning.

Money B founded the famous "Digital Underground" with Tupac Shakur.

Tupac would have turned fifty years old in 2021. Money B told me afterwards about their last private conversation before Tupac was killed in 1996.

It still haunts him.

Money B: The thing I remember most about growing up. My father was in the Black Panther Party, but I actually went to the Oakland Community School. It was a school founded by Huey P. Newton, in Oakland, California. I went there from age like four till I graduated from elementary school age. Because it was a preschool to elementary, even though we did not have first, second, third grades, it was that age group. So, for the most part, my entire elementary years were spent at that school. So, I was raised by members of the Black Panther Party, you know what I mean? So, I always tell people, as a child, I did not know much about the Black Panther Party. But all I knew was the Black Panther Party because that is all I was around. So, I did not know if there was anything else.

I thought everyone grew up that way . . . So, an example of that is, when I got older, right? As we were making records [in] like '88, '89, there was a big movement in hip hop where people [were] wearing dashikis and African medallions and kind of getting to know about Africa and where they came from. I was taught at elementary age about where I came from. I knew about Marcus Garvey, I knew about Malcolm X, we read about Langston Hughes and things like that. Willie Mays came to our school, Rosa Parks visited our school, and it was weird to me that kids went to public school. They did not know about black history until they actually went to college and had to learn on their own. I thought every kid knew what I knew, but I started realizing that they didn't.

We, Rappers, Play Characters . . .Like Pimps and Drug Pushers . . .
I remarked that unlike actors who play other characters, rappers are perceived as expressing their own opinions.

Money B: Rappers are playing characters. Take Too Short, he talks about being a pimp in his music. Right? But he will be the first one to tell you that he is never pimped a day in his life. But you still like to hear him say it, you know what I mean? That Too Short character, you love it. Even though you know he has probably never really done those things that he talks about.

So, for me [it's] loving the culture, loving the art form. I know how to separate that from say, for instance, someone who gets into the music solely to get an opinion across. So, say if I am a rapper and I am like, well, I have these political views that I want to talk about.

I think as a rapper, you should express yourself how you feel. So, if it means something to you say it, but don't say because people expect you to say it.

So, another example. So obviously where I come from and who my dad was. When, I was just getting into the industry with Digital Underground we would make records like *Freaks of the Industry* and some of my songs I am talking about sex. But you know, I am nineteen, twenty years old, I like to drink and have sex, right? So that is, what is on my mind and my dad would be like, "Hey man, you should talk more about this." I'm like, "Yeah. But if you want to have a conversation with me afterwards, I can have these conversations. But I am expressing myself the way that I want to. I have some records when I feel like talking about issues, I will. But right now, I'm talking about this." An artist should not be pressured to do something that does not really feel. Don't talk about being a gangster to try to prove a point, don't talk about political views or social issues if you really are not about that.

Donald Trump Causing Division

We went right to some rappers' opinions about Donald Trump being divisive.

Money B: Coming from where I sit and what I know a lot of people think, it's always been that way. I think now with our so-called leader, right? He's making people feel comfortable to express themselves in a way that they probably always felt, but they just kind of kept it on the low.

He Acts Like a Racist . . .

So, is Donald Trump a racist?!

Money B: I believe that he sides with racists and he acts like a racist. I think Donald Trump probably cares more about money and power than he does about what . . . It could be greed. You know what I mean? Because he speaks to his base, right? If that base were another color, he would still speak to it to stay where he is. Right? But I will say he sounds and seems like a racist without knowing him, because he speaks in racist code. Right? So, when he talks . . . An example that everybody uses, but it is a great example is that. The whole thing with the calling the people, "Fine people." Right? Those are some fine people. Or when there were protests about George Floyd, he would tell the police need to dominate. What does that mean? That means go out and get them. But that . . . people like, "Yeah, go get them."

You know what I mean? So, that creates the separation. The thing about Trump is that he shows no empathy. His message is directly to a specific set of people. The others do not matter.

That is the problem. He does not seem to be a diplomat in any sense of the word. He does not know how to; he does not know how to sit in a room. If you are opposed to him, if you disagree with him, then you are wrong, it is fake, it is not right.

Yeah. He is playing to a specific team and the other team does not matter and I do not think that that is . . . You cannot be a leader of a country by only catering to a specific set of the people.

He is Using the NFL

Yeah and everything is . . . the NFL. He is using everything as . . . I do not even know what the word is. But points for him to bring up like, look at them, they are not kneeling, that is bad. You know what I mean? Get with me because that is bad. You understand? As opposed to let me understand why you guys are doing that? How can we come together? As opposed to calling them sons of bitches. He is divisive.

Me? Talk with Him (Trump)?

I then asked Money B if he would accept an invitation to talk with Trump. He almost fainted.

Money B: To sit in a room with HIM? To talk about anything. Yeah, I would. Only, from what I have seen and from what I know, I do not think a conversation with him would serve anything, you know what I mean? At this point to me he has proven that he is unwilling to listen to different opinions. When did you ever hear fake news, that term, before him? That is a question for you.

When have you seen a president respond in a tweet twenty minutes after anything is ever said about him or that opposes his opinion? Does that sound like somebody who is all of a sudden, he is going to get an epiphany like, okay? What do you want? What do you really think?

Weeks later, Money B would prove that social pressure did not change his commitment to talk with the "other side." I would put him on the phone with then-President Donald Trump. He would go to the White House.

Predicting the Capitol Hill Riots?

And then he added this question regarding: "*What* is going to happen?" Looking back, it was a scary prediction.

Money B: I think it's going to come to a point where there could be real . . . I do not know if it is revolution. I do not know what it is. Like you said, right now, we are so divided. I do not see it coming together anytime soon. The split and the divide is being promoted by people at the top. So, I could see if our president were saying, "Hey, look, we need to come together. Let us figure it out." Right? But he is not doing that. He is just saying look, those people are bad, whatever they say is fake, and dominate. So, what do you think is going to happen?

Glen "Big Baby" Davis

Glen "Big Baby" Davis is known for having played basketball for the Boston Celtics and the Los Angeles Clippers. He is still popular. When he joined us for lunch after the filming at a popular place in Beverly Hills, people jumped to take photos with him. There were couple of Hollywood stars at the restaurant, but Big Baby stole the show and enjoyed it.

Big Baby—like other former sports stars—is trying to figure out his next move.

After retiring from basketball, he wants to explore, "being a foodie": translate his famous love for food, into business.

"I must send you my new BBQ sauce," he told me in such a manner that I started to crave some then and there.

Donald Sterling's Racist Remarks

Racism is not a new topic for him.

He was there when the Donald Sterling scandal broke, and he needed to sell the Clippers due to his racial remarks in 2014 after TMZ published recorded conversations between Sterling and his mistress in which he made racist comments.

Big Baby: I was part of the Clippers. It was not a big surprise for me, because I am from Baton Rouge, Louisiana. And where I am from, it is known for that type of energy. I am used to it. I understand it. I see it. I see the difference. And I am just a guy that is really a soldier on the front line trying to make a difference. When I got into that situation with Sterling, it felt like I have been there before, but it just was sad because to still be stuck in a cycle like that, of that type of energy, when we make you a lot of money as far as just athletes and playing extremely hard, it's sad to see.

Is Donald Trump a Racist?

Is Donald Trump a racist? I do not know. I am going to be honest, because I do not focus on what he says and how he goes about things. I focus on what I can do to help from my side. And what I need to help. How do we build a bridge and how do we translate? Because right now we are all speaking different languages, even though we are speaking English. We are just speaking so many different languages. Everybody is fighting, but I just want to be a teacher to that. And that is the way I look at it. He is our president, and it's United States of America. That is where I live.

It is not united anymore. Yeah, now we need people to translate. We need people to translate, hey, this is not right. We have been talking a long time, but it just has to be more in action. And it is just sad, the things that happen while we are trying to translate and figure this thing out and figure out how to live in this world together. And I just think everything coming to the front, it is just good. And I think there's a process of healing and we've just got to figure it out."

An Open Wound Was Trump Poking Around

I feel like it's a wound that's been opened and Donald Trump is just poking around it. He is not really sticking his hand and digging in yet, but he is poking around that wound and it is bleeding slowly, still a lot of blood oozing. We have just got to figure out how to patch it, how to accept, but at the same time, come to the table to make it better. Accepting that, hey, the ways of back then were then, but the ways that we all have now are different. So, whenever we realize, hey, we are in a different world and we have to accept change. We have to be willing to hear and listen and reteach ourselves the new norm.

I Would Say to Trump: "You Got Big Balls"

Big Baby got colorful. Somehow, even when he criticized Trump, he could not conceal a partial admiration for him. I asked him, if I were to arrange a much-needed meeting, how would Big Baby start it?

Big Baby: Funny but serious at the same time. First of all, I'm going to have to tell him, "You know you got big balls, brother. I respect it." You respect a man and just him and his way of life. Every man is trying to be a king in his own way and Donald Trump, that is his own way. And I respect that. I respect your gangster, man. I respect it. But I think your views and sometimes the things that you portray, you can keep that to yourself. Because I think sometimes, he does not have to react and respond and entertain as much as he does.

He is very entertaining. And then just respect. Have an open mind, sit and be hands-on with people in our community. That is the only way you are going to figure it out. That is the only way you are going to sit and figure out, what can I do for that side? I know what I do for my side, but what can I do for that side? And that is all. Be hands on as much as you can, so you can make your adjustment, not with everybody else. Because one thing that I know that Donald Trump is, he is a hustler. And with our community and hustling, that is all we have ever done. So, how can you break? How can you figure it out?

Mr. Trump, Gumbo Has So Many Different Flavors

I would look at his eyes and say: "Mr. Trump, if you really truly want to understand our culture and who we are, try to be more hands-on in these places, so you can see how you can handle these places. Do not let other people or people around you influence your true instinct of a survivor, a hustler, because those things for our community is where we connect. The hustling part, the entrepreneur part, I respect it. So, let us figure out how we can blend the two.

I am from Louisiana and I love gumbo. But in gumbo, there is so many different flavors. There's crab, there's okra, there's sausage, there is all different types of flavor, but it comes to one. We got to figure out how America tastes as one with so many different flavors. That is what I would say. Figure that out. Figure out how to be a chef, to cater to everybody. Not just one.

Trump, you got to go in these neighborhoods, these people, in spite of what is going on, just to see you there would mean more than anything, because nobody is ever came to Baton Rouge in my neighborhood, or nobody is came to O Block in Chicago, and all these neighborhoods that are having these situations. So be a chef. Be a chef of the country, make us all taste like gumbo."

Eric B

Eric B told anecdotes the way anyone would when they come from the other side of the tracks:

> Because you're not the white man's nigger. These guys in the music business, they talk to the black executives any kind of way.

That was fine with the filmmakers because he was talking at will just like President Trump. There was no No-No rhetoric to worry about with him, either.

Big Problem

When Daphne mentioned to Erbil that they may start filming with Rakim and Eric B, Erbil said that would be great. He talked about the rappers, as if he knew them from Long Island.

For Erbil, anyone from Long Island, New York, or for that matter its extension Queens, was someone from "home." Having lived most of his life in New York, he considered himself one of them despite being born in Turkey.

***

In his encounter with Eric B, Erbil behaved as if they were old friends. But one divide was clear: Eric B was wearing a Yankees hat. Erbil was part of Red Sox Nation.

As noted throughout this book, there is a big divide in America that can never heal. It is like the divide between the Celtics and the Lakers. They are the biggest, yet they are not the only ones. Everyone knows these divisions. They are quite common.

***

But for Erbil this problem had to be resolved before this encounter could continue. He made a point that they were on the same page with Eric B on all outstanding issues involving politics, but they had to resolve the problem of the Yankees hat he was wearing.

That was not acceptable. So, Daphne and Erbil decided to give Eric B a "Trump GameChanger" T-shirt to make it even. Eric B was a good sport and took a photo with Daphne, displaying the T-shirt.

Now, the divides had been handled. It was time to have fun.

First Rapper to Reach Out

On May 25, 2020, a cop put a knee on the neck of a handcuffed black man. Nine horrific minutes later, documented by witnesses on their mobiles, the man died.

The death of George Floyd triggered angry demonstrations and then looting all over America and spread overseas.

It was clear to Bill and me that we could not film a documentary discussing "two Americas" without including in-depth conversations with some rappers and sports figures. Yet we wanted to choose people who have been trusted and respected by the African American community for years.

I first called Eric B.

Eric B and Rakim's album *Paid in Full* was named the greatest hip hop album of all time by MTV in 2006. Born and raised in Queens, New York, Eric B was up to the task. He felt strongly that it was high time to communicate. Painful as it might get, he said, there was no other way.

And yes, even to communicate with Donald Trump.

While Trump's rhetoric offended many African Americans, Eric B believed that the community had to express it to Trump and make him listen. He knew that I had a direct access to Trump and felt I could become a bridge.

So, on a hot summer day, he pulled his car next to the Mark Hotel on New York's Upper East Side.

Our production assistant, Nicole Dicocco, was melting while waiting for Eric B.

Outdoor dining made all of us sweat within minutes, but we were so caught in this discussion that we may unite and create a beginning of a crucial dialogue between Trump's world and some hurt rappers.

He put me on the phone with other rappers, like Killer Mike and Fat Joe.

We were charged.

Racism in the Music Industry

Eric B felt that racism and frustration had started way back when black musicians were used to create great music, but were not allowed to run the labels.

Eric B: "I remember when I first started at MCA, the mob was there. They did not care about color. So, the mob was like, "Look, Eric, you make great records, we got money, we're going to promote it. We're going to make money together." Then the Wall Street guys came in. Then that is when the racial divide came in. They wanted to take over the black music division, so they turned it into the urban division. There's only a handful of black executives now. They changed different black music to urban music. So, if you change it to urban music, you can have a gorilla run it in. When back then everybody was winning when they had black guys running black music. But now when you come in and you take over the whole division and you turn it into urban and you take away the title, black music, now you have no black executives.

There's a big executive. He runs one of the biggest streaming companies and I will not name his name, he said, "Eric, I'm so sick of dealing with these kids and all. Only thing they're worried about is algorithms." And he said, "Music business doesn't have any soul anymore."

Trump, Don King, Mike Tyson, and Me

Eric B actually understands Trump's sometimes insensitive attitude.

He has not seen him for twenty-five years.

Yet he recalled this story: "One thing about Trump, he doesn't care what he says. He is up in age. He has a bunch of money. It is just like Don King. We were talking about Don King earlier. Don King could care less what comes out of his mouth. "I've walked the walk, I've done all these things, I'm just going to say whatever's on my mind." When Mike Tyson used to fight in Atlantic City, Trump was our host. We stayed at his casino. So, it is me, Mike Tyson, and Donald Trump. So, Donald Trump's talking to me one night, it is about three-thirty, four o'clock in the morning. He says, "Eric," he says, "I'm the stupidest guy in the room, but the smartest guy in the room." I said, "Come on, Trump. What does that mean?" So, he says, "Eric, see that guy right there, he has a double Master's. This guy has. . ." And he says, "All of those guys, Eric, work for me." He said, "Eric, don't ever be afraid to hire people that know more than you." And I've lived by that ever since."

Trump? What About the Local Guys?

Eric B believes in being involved in the community. He is serving meals every weekend in a church in Queens. He is involved with Phil Murphy, governor of New Jersey. He thinks healing our society starts close to home.

Eric B: I think it's a big picture. Everybody is focusing on Trump. Trump is one vote. Everybody is worried about Trump, Trump, Trump, but we are letting our local officials slide. Our local senators, our local congressmen. We are letting them slide and giving them a free pass. We are not holding them responsible. I have a saying, "If you are not at the table, you are on the menu." So, we are on the menu. We're sitting up there, "Oh, Trump is the worst. He's a racist, and he needs to get out." But what about our local guys? We are letting them slide. We have forgotten about the basics."

You Will Never Run These Record Companies

Eric B insists that racism is everyday reality.

Eric B: Of course, every day. I had a lawyer by the name of Paul Marshall. One of the greatest lawyers in entertainment. Before he died, he had a conversation with me and he said, "You know what, Eric?" He says, "You know business in your sleep. You got thirty years of experience." But, he said, "You will never, ever, ever be an executive in the music business or run a record company." And I asked him, "Why?" And he said, "Because you're not the white man's nigger. These guys in the music business, they talk to the black executives any kind of way," and he says, "You're not going to entertain that." He said, "They get into arguments with their wives and they belittle and berate them in the staff meetings and this and that," and he says, "You're not the white man's nigger so you'll never run one of these record companies." I could run Def Jam Records in my sleep. But they will put a bunch of other guys in there because they changed it to urban now.

Kneeling During National Anthem

We touched on a subject that Trump turned into a question of being a patriot, though it had started as a protest against the way cops treated black people—Colin Kaepernick kneeling while the national anthem was played.

Eric B: "I mean, I think we go back to the good Reverend Dr. Martin Luther King. Everybody should be able to protest, a quiet protest without violence, and I respect that. I think he took a stance. It is something that was bothering him in his heart. A lot of people do not do that.

But I think it is just like America. America, when they disagreed with somebody they went to war and these guys in the street have gone to war against America. And you cannot sit there and say, "Who's right? Who's wrong?" You know what I am saying? Because America went to war against different countries for their own personal reasons. Now, the war is at their doorstep. I live right there in Brooklyn, right on the Manhattan Bridge, so every day you see they are protesting, they are walking across the bridge, then they are fighting the police, then they are walking with the police. Every day is a different protest.

We Must Have this Uncomfortable Conversation

We've gotten afraid to have that conversation. We have to have an uncomfortable conversation in order for us to understand each other. You and I cannot be on the same page and then think that things are going to get better, where we have somebody else over there that has a different point of view. So, we have to have an uncomfortable conversation to be able to deal with and understand where somebody is coming from. In order to meet somewhere in the middle, we need to have that uncomfortable conversation that we do not want to have.

Calling Out Trump at Awards Shows?

I think every platform when you have is, like I said, you want to have that uncomfortable moment so that people are talking. Like now, so you are talking about it because it was an uncomfortable moment to watch it and you are saying, "Was this the right time for them to say that?" They are like looking at your report card and you are like, "Ah, man." But you have got to have that uncomfortable conversation in order for everybody to understand each other.

Actually, a lot of people do not understand it. The track, it came from James Brown, the "Funky President" so they call it Eric B is president. We do not look at them as white rappers, we look at them as just entertainment.

Kid Rock's a white rapper, Donnie Wahlberg is a white pop singer. They are our friends and family because we grew up with them.

Democrat with an Open Mind

Eric B is not thrilled about being described as "supporting" this candidate or another.

"I mean, that's what it's about. And you want your friends to actually support what you support. Just like the Republican Party. Democrats always talk about this, "Oh, we're together, brother, we're with you, we're with you." Not going to happen. They asked me, "Eric, are you a Democrat?" And I said, "No, I'm a Democrat with an open mind."

I said, "Try that one." I said, "I'm a Democrat with an open mind." The majority of Democrats when you deal with them, these guys, they are not stand-up people. And that's why Trump was able to run right over them. I will never forget. I was watching CNN in the house and I remember they were like, "Trump will never win. He has to win here, here, here, here, here, here, here, here, here, here, here, and here. He'll never win." Came back from commercial, everybody was sweating, looking crazy. I said, "What just happened?" "This is just in," and they do not stick to the plan. One thing about Republicans, they stick together regardless to what the problem is, they will talk about it behind the scenes, but they stick together and have a united front.

We All Have to Unite

"I mean, we all have to unite. We all have to just put down our shields for a second and just listen, have that uncomfortable conversation. Talk with each other not at each other. I think if I had to sit home and not do nothing, like every time somebody calls me, they are like, "Eric, what are you doing?" "I'm sitting on the couch watching CNN." Like, it kills me. I am sitting I am like, "Wow, can I just go out to work and do something instead of two separate Americas?" Like I said before, we have to sit there and actually have that uncomfortable conversation."

If Only Trump Apologized for the Central Park Five!

Eric B is convinced that he found the key to break years of anger and start a productive dialogue. If only, he told me, Donald Trump would apologize for the Central Park Five.

In 1989, Trump bought newspaper advertisements and called for New York State to adopt the death penalty in the light of a rape in the park in which a jogger was killed.

Later, it would be revealed that the five black and Latino men were wrongly convicted of the brutal crime. He feels strongly that this apology would do the trick.

Eric B: I'd have a conversation with Trump [and] might say, "You know what? Trump, you need to apologize for the Central Park Five. You know you were wrong. Just say that, 'Somebody guided me.'" When he did the article about the Central Park Five and stuff like that. "Now you see all this stuff has come out. You were wrong and then start from there."

***

Trump has been known for not apologizing. Yet Eric B did not see the big deal.

Eric B: Hey, he figured out just like everybody else, "If I'm wrong, I'm wrong. I got to be honest and say, 'Hey, I made a mistake, and I was wrong.'" In the black community, if Donald Trump sat there and said, "Hey, I would like to apologize to the Central Park Five, I'm going to bring them and their families up to the White House. We're going to sit down and have a conversation," that right there is the uncomfortable conversation that I'm talking about. People are going to say, "Hey, y'all, he's not that bad as we thought he was. He came back and atoned for what he did."

Trump, this is a simple stuff that you do. It is simple. It does not take a rocket scientist to figure it out. Everybody is trying to come up with all these big ways and it is . . . It is simple. We have gotten away from simple, simple stuff. I have wronged you, my sister, I am sorry, and I apologize. How does that hurt you?

***

We finished the interview with such a great feeling: there *is* a way forward where both sides can meet.

And as we would all find out, that *easy* is not a word which is remotely relevant to the difficult, hard feelings between the two sides.

CHAPTER FOUR

Two Americas

W hen all was said and done, the fact that there was two Americas became apparent to the filmmakers. They had already identified the "culprits." There was also two main scape-goats like discrimination and racism.

While some were focusing on talking about their fears and anxieties, the other side was insisting that the show must go on, business as usual.

Robert Davi and Kristy Swanson talked about fears and anxieties. While Robert complained about not getting calls from Hollywood, Kristy was also trying to look hopeful, posing the question, "Can we get along?"

Mark Geragos and Avi Lerner talked as if there was no toxic political or biological environment around. One was in his office in Los Angeles busy as usual, the other was all over the world filming like any other day.

Fears and Anxieties

Fears and anxieties varied from one interviewee to another. While some were fearful of losing Hollywood jobs, others showed no concern and wished that the toxic political atmosphere would subside sooner than later.

Others, rappers in particular, have talked about a clear racial divide that exists in the country. Two of them talked about their fears about members of the law enforcement. They said that they were afraid to go out one day and come across a racist person that will come after them.

Next to the toxic political environment, practically no one talked about COVID-19 first and foremost. It was always a secondary fear or anxiety for them. Perhaps for the conservatives, COVID-19 was a fabricated problem, but liberals also did not bring it up as a primary source of problem in America.

Trump persona and racism were the most important issues for all of them. Those that were pro-Trump had their fear focused on the behavior of the Hollywood elite and issues like socialism and communism. Those against him pointed at President Trump himself when it came to the source of their anxiety. Their fears varied from one to another.

Robert Davi

Anxiety was clear with Robert Davi. Aside from the divide between President Trump and Hollywood, there was also anxiety about COVID-19. He was most worried about the lost opportunities in filmmaking.

Supporting Trump hurt my career.

—Robert Davi

Worrying about his family was equally formidable. Above all, he had a little baby at home to worry about.

The interview with Robert Davi was filmed at his home. This was a first. Until then, there were only studio and hotel shoots.

Going to a residence was always tricky anyway. The interviewee had the upper hand with many aspects. The filmmakers needed to accommodate the host.

In this case, this was Los Angeles. Noise was a factor. A car or a plane was plenty to disrupt filming unless it was soundproof.

When they filmed with Kevin and Sam in Palm Beach, they were indoors. Yet, the ferocious rain was equally destructive. At the Davi residence, the conditions were even more sensitive. They were filming outside in the backyard.

At Home with Robert Davi, Rather in the Backyard

Robert Davi received us at his home in LA with his young wife, Diana, and their baby, Gabriela Nicole. It was early days of the new reality of COVID-19. We were trying to abide by the rules.

So, we stuck to filming in his yard. He prepared coffee and pastry and had his son Nick assisting.

He has appeared in more than 130 films. He is also a good crooner. His record *Davi Sings Sinatra* was a hit.

While we were filming, he was preparing for his next role in a Reagan biopic, playing late Soviet leader Leonid Brezhnev.

So, when I asked him to compare Hollywood's treatment towards Ronald Reagan and Donald Trump, he dived right in, adding historical facts and perspective.

Talking About Reagan. . .

Robert Davi: He was very . . . Well, first off, Reagan had an interesting history because he considered himself a bleeding-heart liberal initially, back in the forties, when he was part of the Hollywood community. And so, he was on the inside of the AFL-CIO and all those union things that were happening. For the betterment of mankind. And then he realized at a certain point that the Communist Party had infiltrated the unions and other aspects, and that they were being manipulated and used as pawns. And this is in the forties.

And there was an actress, let us say the Meryl Streep of her day, Ida Lupino. She was a director, brilliant actress, one of the first women in film. And she had a meeting at her house that was called by a guy named Sterling Hayden, who was the police captain in *The Godfather*, the one that punched out Pacino. Now Sterling Hayden was a war veteran, good American, but he was also a communist sympathizer. And he had a meeting of the Communist Party at Ida Lupino's house in Hollywood.

William Holden told Ronald Reagan about this meeting, and Reagan went to the meeting and kind of crashed it, and he wanted to speak to them. And all the Hollywood, you know, and Ronald Reagan shows up, and he wants to speak, and they are shouting him down.

John Garfield stood up and said, "He should speak. We should let him speak. He has a right to speak. We should let him speak."

Well, Howard De Silva then took John Garfield outside and berated the hell out of him. Why did you? And Reagan then went and spoke to the Hollywood community for forty-five minutes or more.

Years later, Sterling Hayden, who then left the socialist idealism, said that Ronald Reagan was a one-man wrecking crew. Just think about that. Think about the infiltration of Hollywood by the Communist Party, back in the forties and fifties, which was a very real thing. They had people in the agencies reading scripts, in the studios reading scripts. So, if a social agenda was pregnant with some of the things, they wanted to put forward, it was moved up. Other things were moved away.

So cut to Ronald Reagan, SAG [Screen Actor's Guild], governor of California, tough going, great communicator, but what Reagan had to do with men like Frank Sinatra and Gregory Peck, and huge Hollywood stars that were for him, as well as the people that were opposing him when he ran for president.

So, the vitriol against Ronald Reagan was tremendous inside the parties, but Reagan, because it is the populist movement and the people, much like what Donald Trump did, overrode that and became president of the United States.

Now, the odd thing to it is you have Reagan's success in terms of "Mister Gorbachev tear down this wall." And the Berlin Wall comes down. And his alliance with Margaret Thatcher, and the Pope John Paul. Communism is defeated, is . . . . Which was really established a little bit earlier, you know, with Brezhnev. Brezhnev was working toward that a little bit. And Reagan met Brezhnev at Nixon's party that he had for him. This is back in the seventies. So, they had a relationship.

The interesting thing about Brezhnev, and there were letters written to Reagan and Brezhnev. Brezhnev, there was an assassination attempt on Brezhnev in [1969], by one of the drivers. They missed. When Reagan was [shot at in an attempted assassination], that is when the thawing started to happen. So, I suspect, in some strange way, that . . . because Reagan wrote a letter to Brezhnev, and the response from Brezhnev was much warmer. I think the [failed] assassinations that the two may have felt at the time could have been a bridge to both. Who knows? But it was set up that way. Had Brezhnev lived there would have been a meeting with Reagan. As it went, it was Gorbachev. So, he brings down the Berlin Wall. And what happens?

In 1988, George Bush runs for president. And what is his slogan? You remember the slogan? The slogan is a kinder, gentler nation. Now, I look at that and I go, you are my right-hand guy. You saw what we did in the world. The economy is growing. We now defeated communism. The Cold War is over. And you are saying, and I do not want to use a crude term, but you are crapping on my presidency by saying a kinder, gentler nation? As if what I did, peace through strength is no good? What we did as my right-hand guy, what we did is now we are going to negate this? This is the start of the globalists. This is part of a global assessment if you will.

So, you had Bush. Then you had Clinton. And then Bush two. And then Obama. And it is all uphill. I mean, it is an astounding thing. And so, Reagan had that heart who protected

him, like I said, in the Hollywood community, you had big stars
that were able to counteract all the vitriol. Even take a simple
thing like the Star Wars defense, which is real hazmat. Reagan
had won. The Star Wars defense system. Now, what is interesting about Reagan in the Star Wars defense, and because he had
imagination. Like Trump, he had an impulse and instinct. Trump
has an instinct like that when that first wave of migration was
happening, and he saw all everyone saw on the news, all the
young men that should be fighting for their country are coming
across the border. What is that all about?

And if you read Oriana Fallaci's book, *The Force of Reason*—
it is a great book; you should read that—she was one of the first
voices of the west to say that they were paying young people to
come to migrate to and she was the first one to call it Arabia.

Blacklisting in Hollywood: Then and Now

Right. And we must clear that up. You see, I think this is really
what is needed. Because so many times over this era of Russia,
and what has been happening to the conservative people in
Hollywood and throughout media, the new blacklist. The new
McCarthy era. Even GOP politicians refer to it as the McCarthy
era. There was a thing called the Venona Project. You ever hear
of that? Let me tell you.

The Venona Project was a Soviet code that the Soviets
thought was undecipherable, that we could not decode it
since the thirties. But guess what? We had. We decoded it. So,
what happens is 99 percent of the people Joe McCarthy fingered
as communist in our government—Secretary of Treasury for
Roosevelt. Communist. Head of the *New York Times*. Communist.
People that they fingered. So, when they say it is the McCarthy
era, no it is not. Because McCarthy was somewhat exonerated
by the Venona Project in 1996.

That was the House Un-American Activities [Committee]
that went on a fishing expedition. That was another thing.

That is what I am saying, there are two different things. And there was a huge blacklist, of course. Kirk Douglas was the first one along with Sinatra to break the blacklist. You know, he hired [Dalton Trumbo] to write *Spartacus*. One, I think, of the great writers. Absolutely there was a blacklist. Back in the day. And you would think, with all the films, and all the discussion about how bad the blacklisting is, because it is. Freedom of speech and freedom of thought and freedom of everything else should not be blacklisted. You know, what they are doing today is they are stapling people's tongues to their foreheads, I say. And the black-list in Hollywood, like you said, with Debra Messing and other people tweeting about, let us find out who is voting for Trump.

And other people De Niro came out and said the other day, you got to be an idiot to vote for Trump. They are now denigrat-ing the voters. You are racist. You are this. And this is an inter-esting thing because celebrity does have influence. And I know this as a kid. When I was a kid and Dean Martin or Frank Sinatra or Joey Bishop, or Alan King, or somebody was liking some polit-ical figure, I was more apt to be sympathetic to that ideology than an opposing, only because of the celebrities. So, there is a lot of kids that have no clue that are following that paradigm.

Reagan Gave a Medal to Trump's Uncle

I must give you a little bit of bona fides because since the sixties me and my cousin used to follow politics and used to have a tape recorder. And do our own political commentary and imperson-ations. So, we had my family who were Kennedy Democrats, and his family, his father was a conservative. And then we would switch sides. We would play this game with each other. And then arguably, this is young kids eleven years old doing this. And, you know, also encouraged by the uncle. My uncle was very political. And so, we then I think, over the years, being aware and being understanding, my father gave me a book. When I was about eleven years old. He was a Knight of Columbus. He gave me two books. One was called *Masters of Deceit*, by J. Edgar Hoover. And the other was called *None Dare Call It Treason*.

Now *None Dare Call It Treason* was written by John Stormer, who was allegedly a John Bircher and had a bad connotation. But I read in that book, the prophecy of what was happening to America, and how social Marxist culturalism was going to affect the nation on all aspects, and what their agenda was. Now, if you are a young kid, eleven years old, and you read this; he said, "Just read these." Those are the only two books he ever gave me. My father, "Just read these for me." I read them and that was it. But over the years, I have got six kids, over multiple generations looking at education. Looking at the infiltration of education of common core, of what they were doing. And then politics and the movement.

And then at a certain point, it just all just lined up like a slot machine in my brain. What was happening with the globalists in America? Now, I have known about Trump for years. I know what he did with Wollman Rink, New York, Queens, Astoria. And we were talking about the Star Wars defense. And it is interesting for that because John Trump, Fred Trump's brother, I do not know if you know, this was the head of MIT. You probably know, forty years. Forty years John Trump was the head of MIT.

Reagan gave him the Medal of Freedom. John Trump. Trump was in the office when he got it. Now, that is an intelligent human being MIT. Not only that, the Star Wars defense. Not only that, the CIA, when Nikola Tesla died, the CIA brought to John Trump, Donald's uncle, all of Nikola's papers. All the stuff they took out of his safe and says what is he working on? And John Trump had many inventions.

You know, people were saying, I mean, the day he came down on June 15, I wrote the article for Breitbart that he was the candidate, he was going to win.

And every subsequent, I wrote about thirty-five articles, why he was going to win when they were saying he was not going to win. And they had [Ted] Cruz and [Marco] Rubio and they had seventeen candidates, and I was just saying, "There's no way they're going to win." Because on Breitbart, and over the years, I have been writing articles, dealing with immigration, dealing with China, dealing with all kinds of articles, so I knew this. I had a meeting with Mitch McConnell in 2010 when I wrote the article about immigration, begging him to please take [on] immigration. Start doing something about immigration. Much like I am wondering why they are not doing anything about [Adam] Schiff. The Senate Intelligence Committee has the power to investigate what is happening with Schiff and Russiagate. If everything is a bogus thing, and Schiff . . . I just saw all the clips with Schiff going, yes, there's Russian collusion. And he goes, "You mean to tell me these congressmen and these senators are like the Royal Roman Senate?"

[In America] I thought the individual was the leader. Now these guys are commissars. I see them as commissars. I see them in Roman togas. Corrupters, all right, of Caesar's senate. And then the knives are out to stab them on the steps of the Capitol Building, or in the front of the Lincoln Memorial, which they did when he gave a speech on that. You know, he was a guy, Donald Trump. I remember in Hollywood, and I will not mention the stars' names, but everyone in the eighties was reading *The Art of The Deal*. And looking at buildings and going, "Yeah, I want to do like that and I want to be like, you know, he is terrific and Donald Trump. Yeah." I mean all of them, even the rappers. Everybody.

Now suddenly, and what he said on *Oprah* twenty years ago, twenty-five years ago and *Phil Donahue* has not changed.

We are sitting there knowing that we have been duped by our politicians into this. Ross Perot was the first crack in the egg. And when you think what happened to Ross Perot, he leaves. Because he probably foresaw what was going to happen. Trump, it is just astounding. I do not think any other person could be still, they would have resigned, they would have taken a way out. This guy has the fortitude and the belief of it despite all the criticisms. No human being is perfect. I am tired of all that nonsense about the tweeting. I enjoy the tweeting. It keeps you on your toes. Now Coronavirus. And people complaining about that because no one, I do not care who is in the administration, there was going to be issues.

I travel the world and I travel the country. I consider myself, not an elitist, the man of the people. So, I communicate. So, I sensed with Donald Trump's message meant to the forgotten man. I sent it on Neil Cavuto a year before they used it. The forgotten man, you could find that article when I said that. I said, "Neil, there is a group of people in this nation that they feel ignored." You can find them I will send you the article. But they feel ignored. And a year later forgotten man came.

Now, so you go [on] Fox News and Breitbart and you say, "Well, I support Donald Trump." At that point there are many other candidates for the Republican Party. I had couple of billionaires trying to convince me not to support him, which I continue to support him, but you know, I mean for the consensus of the Republican Party, what is the response when you make this announcement from Hollywood first? Agents, friends, directors?

Well, the response, even from my friends in the community that were conservative. What are you nuts? They were either Rubio or Cruz or Bush. They were, you know, what are you nuts, [John] Kasich. I mean, and I was now fighting that. So now I was ostracized from my conservative community. And I was writing these freaking articles, you know, and, you know that every man was supporting it. But the Hollywood community then, I think now, that was the conservative. Outside the conservative movement in the liberal establishment of Hollywood, it was not an effect because they never thought he was going to win. So they would throw it off and dismiss it. You know what I mean? Come on, you cannot really be voting for this guy. You know what I mean? Or I would get a phone call when a mishap would happen that they thought would take him out. They'd go "All right, are you ready to renounce him now?"

It is brilliant. That is why I bring up Trump. The guy has a brilliant mind, and you must let him do what he is going to do. You know, I mean, let him do what he is going to do. There it is. You know, the politics of it he changes and . . . well . . . he just fired this inspector general. He just fired that guy there. All right. If you do not find the right CEOs, what are you going to do?

Imagine if they did not do that, what he would have been able to accomplish. Look at immigration. Immigration, they yelled and moaned, and this and that. And they are phony about it. What is amazing to me is that they all wanted the same thing. That is what was astounding. See, I thought Trump was going to really get both the left and the right. Because the left was saying the same stuff. Build the wall. Remember [Chuck] Schumer and Clinton and everybody saying the same thing?

Supporting Trump Hurt My Career

It affected it. I know things have. I know, people have recommended me for a film. And the guy said to this other person, "I would love to use him. He's a great actor, but they'd never let me use him." And I have heard that a couple of times. Now, other jobs I have had, you know, sometimes. And my agent says, "Hey, they'll call me up." My manager. "Hey, they made an offer, you know, they're going to make an offer on this." And then the TV series called *Blacklist*. You want to talk about *Blacklist*? People on that show wanted me on the show, but for some reason, it never happened.

I could not do anything that my heart does not say. It is not about the money. As much as it hurts. Look at the world right now. People are suffering all over. They did not vote for Trump.

They voted for Trump. You never know what about life. And all you can do is live it as truthfully as you believe. You know, and as you evolve. And you trust in God. You know, you trust in God and hopefully there . . . And there are people out there that you know it does not matter to, what things happen. But I thought about that question, believe me. That was a question.

GOP: *Ungracious, Kevin McCarthy Never Invited Me*

And what affects me more than that is the deafness from the right. The disrespect from the GOP. Now, I am not blowing my own horn, but I am a good actor. I am a terrific singer.

I've done more than a hundred movies . . . And my music. And I have done some iconic pictures that face the millennials. You know, when you have *Goonies* and Bond and this and *Die Hard*, you are in the consciousness of kids through generations. it is not like you did something twenty-five years ago, and you are still you know, an expendable. You know, I am still doing stuff, thank God, and my singing. Around the world, to sold out concerts. I am never asked to sing. That is what hurts more than anything. Because what that does, that increases your own profile. And once your own profile is increased, then you have a buffer to the blacklist of Hollywood in some way. And that is where it is really, I cannot think of strong enough words. My disappointment in that because it is totally, it has no loyalty. And it should.

How could you send it to Donald Trump? You cannot send it to Donald Trump. You know, people told me "Oh, we spoke to Donald Trump, he likes you." Or this or that or the other. He tweeted one of my articles before he won. I was told "Yeah, you're going to be invited to the inauguration." Nothing. And it is not even about that. It is about the country and about the beliefs. But part of my own selfishness, for my supportive family, is the lack of support that I get for putting myself there. And that is not why you are doing it. You know what I am saying in the first place. But you do hope as a human being that there is some residual appreciation. Because again, like I said, I am going to play you a Christmas song I did. They would not even play it at Christmas. Okay, at the White House. Now somebody in there is blocking, whatever it is. I will just be frank. Does it bother me? Yes, it bothers me. Just like it would bother him.

The same thing that happened when he did the Wollman Rink, if you remember the Wollman Rink. Now, this is an important story. And I had written about it. Nineteen eighty. Mayor Koch, the city parks department want to redo, renovate Wollman Rink. Okay? $3 million in two years.. Get this. Two years go by, a little girl looking out the park window says "Daddy, when is the rink going to be ready?" Probably soon honey. Four years. $6 million. Okay, how about this now? Six years and nine, whatever it be, nine million. Daddy, when is the—? He says, "What the heck's going on?" He goes down. He speaks to Koch. Koch says we need another two years. So, twelve years. He goes, "What?" [Trump] says, "Let me take it over."

So, he takes over the Wollman Rink. There was a big war in the press. Now, what he had done to the Commodore Hotel in New York City and some other areas. Him and [Mayor] Giuliani helped, you know, clean up New York in that time. So now he takes the Wollman Rink, and does it in four months, and saves like about $800,000. And it was, he said, if I went over, I would be out of his pocket. And if it was not, then they go to the charity of cerebral palsy, AIDS victims, and the homeless. He did it four months. The first thing he did was he said, "Who designed this rink?" A refrigeration expert from Florida. Now, this is the common-sense Trump. And this is one of the reasons why I wanted him because I know our infrastructure was crumbling. Right?

So, he goes, "What's this refrigeration expert know about an ice rink?" So, he calls up the Montreal Canadiens. He says, "Who built the rink?" So, and so, who builds your rinks for them? I want to talk to him. He gets the guy; the guy comes down, looks at Central Park. Now, he goes, "Well, first thing is the . . . . They're using copper tubing." You do not use copper tubing. Now what they were doing was they were putting copper tubing down, and then it would be stolen. So, the graft. That is why when we see in the 405 freeway, these guys are building for months and months and months and years and years and years and money is going wasted.

It is like the airport they want to build and 300 you know, anyway. Bottom line is he knows infrastructure. He knows how to save money like he did with the embassy in Israel. He can do that. He could do that for our nation. And I think they understood that the game would be over with a guy like Donald Trump in office. Much like they were afraid with Ross Perot. Because Ross Perot said, "I have to get underneath the hood and see what's happening."

Trump a Racist?

The interview with Davi took place before the chilling video of George Floyd's murder.

Robert Davi was shocked. He kept calling me, concerned that his remarks about racism should be filmed again. He felt strong, it was time to address racism, as an artist, as an American.

He had some constructive ideas: "Tell Trump to invite African Americans from both sides of the aisle . . . If someone doesn't accept, it is on him (or her) . . . But he must address what is going on." Demonstrations were filling the streets, all over the country. It spread fast and turned into violence and looting.

Davi could hear the angry crowd from his home, but fear did not take over. He wanted to do something and start a dialogue.

Here is what he said prior to Floyd's death:

"Donald. Okay. Donald Trump is a racist? . . . Now, friend of mine, a doctor in New York. Cardiologist. Was the cardiologist of a man who was the doorman for Trump. For twenty years, fifteen years. Irish immigrant. His son's a New York City cop.

Daphne Barak and Erbil Gunasti with their Japanese hosts in Yokohama, a few weeks before filming their *Trump vs. Hollywood* documentary.

Daphne and Erbil on a private dinner cruiser with Covid-19 infested *Corona Princess* cruise ship docked on the Yokohama harbor that quickly became a tourist attraction.

Violinist noticing that she is not the main attraction during her performance at a private dinner for Daphne and Erbil.

Shemane and Ted Nugent with Daphne at their ranch in Texas during filming for the documentary. Zebra carpet is a kill by Shemane in Africa with a bow and arrow.

Daphne and Erbil with Sam and Kevin Sorbo at the Brazilian Court Hotel in Palm Beach, Florida, during the looting crisis, resultant curfews, and following the death of George Floyd.

Daphne and Erbil with Dean Cain in the company of their filming crew, headed by Monica and Tim Carney. Tim filmed most interviews to carefully mitigate the effects of the pandemic.

Daphne and Erbil with Scott Baio, the first of the twenty-four interviews for the documentary, filmed in a Los Angeles studio chosen by Scott. Easing the fear of the pandemic was always a priority for the filmmakers.

Brother of Julia Roberts and father of Emma Roberts, Eric—with his wife Eliza—were part of the documentary. They opened their LA home to us for filming.

Daphne and Erbil with Lorenzo Lamas at the Bungalows of the Beverly Hills Hotel, posing with filmmakers' books.

Rapper Too Short with Daphne at the Polo Lounge of the Beverly Hills Hotel, having lunch after filming a moving interview for the documentary.

Glen "Big Baby" Davis of Boston Celtics and LA Clippers with Daphne at the Polo Lounge, enjoying a respite from fans coming for autographs.

Rapper Eric B filming with Daphne at the Mark Hotel in New York, one of the handful luxury hospitality that was partially open during the pandemic months.

Isiah Washington and Daphne with Tim and Jamie, wife of Steven Paul (Jon Voight's partner). Filming at their studio in Beverly Hills.

Claudia Jordan and Daphne in front of the Bungalows at the Beverly Hills Hotel, after she expressed her disappointment about a once-close friendship with Donald Trump.

Kristy Swanson with Daphne and Erbil at the Willard Hotel. The famous and historic DC spot was open only with two floors and no room service or other hospitality.

Erbil with Mama Sarah Obama, paternal grandmother of the 44th President of the United States, Barack Obama, in Kenya.

Daphne with Mama Saraha Obama during the first of her two visits, deep in black Africa, at her home in Kogelo, Kenya.

Daphne and Erbil with famous lawyer of Hollywood stars and entertainers, Mark Geragos, in his Los Angeles office when downtown was deserted.

Hollywood's powerful producer with more than 400 movies, Avi Lerner, at home with Daphne, filming for the documentary.

Robert Davi, who has done more than a hundred movies, filming at his home with Daphne for the documentary.

Rick Gates, who was Deputy Campaign Manager of then-candidate Donald Trump and later Deputy of the Chairman of the Trump Inauguration, filming with Daphne.

Jon Voight with Daphne in 2017, when she introduced Jon in Los Angeles to then Crown Prince Philip, who became King of Belgium a few weeks later.

Jon Voight and Roseanne Barr, with Erbil, a few weeks before filming *Trump vs. Hollywood*, after lunch at Nobu in Malibu.

Daphne and Erbil, heading to one of their regular lunches in Palm Beach, Florida, during a trip when they also visited with President Trump.

The logo of the *Trump vs. Hollywood* documentary prior to the November 3, 2020, presidential election.

The revised version of the logo for the *Trump vs. Hollywood* documentary, when on November 4, election results were not yet announced.

Rapper Money B with Daphne filming for the documentary at the residence of the filmmakers in the California desert.

Daphne and Money B with Texas Governor Gregg Abott at the White House Christmas Party.

The last Chief of Staff of the Trump Administration, Mark Meadows, with Daphne and Money B at the White House Christmas Party.

Daphne and President Trump, during a relaxing weekend in Palm Beach, posing for Erbil, taking a break from lunch and golfing.

Daphne and First Lady Melania Trump, at Mar-a-Lago, chatting after one of the regular night out dinners.

Daphne at the White House Christmas Party, specially invited by President Trump, to celebrate the release of their documentary, *Trump vs. Hollywood*.

Daphne and Erbil with close friends Bettina and Jimmy, having fun with a selfie at the White House Christmas Party.

Daphne and Erbil, enjoying a private moment with delicacies from the White House kitchen during the Christmas Party.

Sevim Gunasti, Erbil's mother, was very instrumental in the making of the *Trump vs. Hollywood* documentary with her prayers—so much so that US Congressman Darrell Issa called to make sure she was mentioned for her contributions.

That doctor talked to the doorman about Trump. He goes, "Tell me about Donald Trump." He goes, "He would give you the shirt off his back." What? Yeah, he literally gave me the shirt off his back.

What about racism? He goes, "What?" He goes, "We used to call the locker room for Trump Tower the League of Nations because there was no color, no race." What else did he tell you? He told me that one time, Donald comes in the building wherever it might be, and he sees a group of kids reading books over here, another group over there. A couple of days later the same thing. He said, "John. What is it? What are they doing?" Oh, they are studying for the exams, Mr. Trump. College. Studying for exams. Two days later, he says, "If they want to study there, they should have a good place to study. They don't have to do it out here."

Cab drivers, limo drivers, people in New York. 'Cause I was from New York. So, when he ran and I was supporting him, I then started to sniff around myself. Asking people about Trump. Pakistani cab driver who was a limo guy, did you ever drive Donald Trump? Amazing. No racism, no racism. Six years before he ran, he had all the black pastors in there, wanting to know what is with the inner city? He got the NAACP award with Jesse Jackson. Now suddenly, he is racist. Suddenly, the narrative changes. All right? Because of corruption. Because they knew this guy. Look it up.

What did he do? He has got a great group of guys with urban revitalization. We have seen the same crap over and over in the inner cities. Chicago. The deaths. The black-on-black deaths. Detroit. I filmed in Detroit many times. It looked like a decayed tooth. He hates ugliness. Is there something wrong with that, in wanting to make America as good as it can be? And to help all the people? Minorities? He is not racist. Is he America first? Yes. If that is racist, then I am a racist. And anyone that cares about our nation's a racist. And that is all because of the globalists. That is the Marxist cultural agenda.

The Marxist cultural agenda is to separate people. Ferguson was a turning point in our nation. President Obama should have united the nation during Ferguson. He did not. They made more of a separation. There was a time to bring it together. But that is not the cultural agenda of the Marxists. They are to split the groups off, so you start backbiting each other and creating chaos. Which is what they've been doing.

De Niro: "Five Minutes with Obama"

The one name every conservative entertainer has to weigh in on is Robert De Niro. His anti-Trump remarks have become part of the Trump vs. Hollywood saga.

Davi was captured by *TMZ* cameras using a strong language after De Niro's famous "F. . . Trump." He reacted: "I respect you as an actor, but it was disgusting what you did, and everyone who stood up."

Robert: Robert De Niro, who I've met. Now when De Niro did the thing at the Tony Awards, I came off the plane at midnight from New York. And someone captured.

TMZ got it. I was like, I am tired. 12:30. First thing in my face is a camera. And that is how I felt. And that is how I still feel. I did not agree with President Obama on everything. But I never disrespected him. I wrote an article called "Five Minutes with Obama." With the Washington *The Hill*. If you will have a grievance, be intellectual with your grievance. You are making it personal in a different way. Even if it goes there. I think it probably has some land deals that they had. Who the hell knows? I think the feud between Trump and De Niro go back, go back, go back who knows where? There is too much vitriol there.

Yeah.

You are being attacked and it's fair game. See, I believe, in ancient Rome, and I begged them to do this. I also spoke about this [at] CPAC [Conservative Political Action Conference].

Ancient Rome had the [Calumnia]. Ancient Rome. That was because good upstanding people were running for political office. And those good people were then slandered. They made up stories. What LBJ did one time. He said to his campaign manager, "Float this story that he's a pedophile, my opponent's a pedophile." And the campaign guy says, "Mr. Johnson that's not true." He says, "I know that. I just want to see him deny it."

So, [Calumnia], where good upstanding people were accused of different things. Now if it were found, like Adam Schiff, that what you accused someone of, you would have to suffer the punishment of what you accused that person of. We should bring that back. I want ancient Rome's [Calumnia] law because I think people would think twice and bite their tongue before they went accusing. Because we have to do something with this current situation.

Pelosi Introduced Me to Obama

It is an interesting premise. And it could be. There could be truth to that premise in some way. I do not know for sure. Beyond the ideology. The ideology of the left. You know. And it is so ingrained, that I do not think the ego of it is of that specific thing. I think it is such an ingrained kind of religion of the left that is something else. Because when you had a couple of those actresses screaming in Washington DC, the ugliest things. And say poetry that is so, so, it was just too inelegant and harsh. I mean, and what is the reason for it?

See that is irrational. Madonna blowing up the White House. Again, I mean, right now, I have said things about Nancy Pelosi because I do not like what she has been doing. I do not like the line of the left. If you are going to say I wanted border control, do not suddenly say you do not want it for the expediency of gerrymandering the population. Because that is all it is. It is bringing people here that do not understand our nation. Along with what the educational process is. Because it is convenient for you to change your point of view about immigration.

You need borders. A country needs that. It is like a house without walls. There is nothing. There is nothing. So, Pelosi. Now I met Pelosi through a guy named Joe Cerrell who was a Kennedy lobbyist and a great man. He was president of the National Italian American Foundation. And he was a Democratic lobbyist, or PR guy. Knew everybody. And when I was with Safe America, internet safety for kids, the first program, 1998. Now with Joe, a good idea trumped politics. And being Italian American trumped politics. If you had both, you were in. So, I am Italian, and he was Italian American.

So now when he passed on, the family wanted me to give his represent thing. So, I spoke about Joe Cerrell. He was a great man. Dutch uncle to me. And Nancy Pelosi spoke. And I said in my speech, "Speaker Pelosi I want to tell you that most people," and a lot of Hollywood were in the audience, "know we don't see eye to eye on politics. But I want to say how proud we are of you being the first speaker of the house. And the first Italian American speaker of the house. In the spirit of Joe Cerrell." And I said about the good idea.

So, after the thing she was so sweet. Real charming. Not like she comes across on TV. Very warm, very nice. A year later I do this article, "Five Minutes with Obama." And I tell him he should support Israel. My ideas if I had five minutes, here Mr. President, here is what I suggest. And at the end I said, "You know, Mr. President it's customary for those in the White House to invite like-minded celebrities. Why don't you break with that tradition and invite some of us who don't see eye to eye and hear what we have to say." I go, "Better yet, why don't you meet with me and some of my friends in Astoria, Queens, where I grew up."

This article came out on a Friday. Now in Washington, DC, every year there is a big crème de la crème of the Italian community. And the president always goes to these dinners. But Obama had not been to one yet. President Obama had not been to one yet after three years. Or four years, whatever it was. My article comes out. Astoria, Queens. They tell me he is not coming to the thing. Because you [need] security clearance. That Wednesday, now the event's on a Saturday night, I get a phone call. The president is coming. What?

Now my ego goes, he read my article. Why don't you come and meet with me and some of my friends in Astoria, Queens? My ego. He read my article. Wow. He is coming to it. Saturday night comes. Now there is three daises. [A] Supreme Court Justice is in the front dais with Nancy Pelosi, politicians. And here is the dais, here is the speaking thing. You got celebrities like me and Sophia Loren might be [there]. And then you have the other businessmen. Three tiers. And there are three thousand people.

President Obama comes on to speak. Gives a great speech about the Italian immigrant contribution to America. Gets a standing ovation. Nancy Pelosi, who was next to the podium, as the president is waving, turns around and looks backwards. She is looking up and down the daises. She sees me. She walks over to where I am, which is not next to her. She goes, "Robert, give me your hand." Takes my hand, over everybody's head, other celebrities. To the middle of the room. And she goes, "Mr. President. Mr. President. It's Robert Davi."

And President Obama turns around and looks at me and goes. "Robert Davi. You're a great actor." God bless you, Mr. President. Now how interesting is that? How interesting is that? Another night Bill Clinton comes. And I have got the pictures. And he comes, and he shakes my hand. He goes, "Robert Davi," he says, "you're a great actor. I watch all your movies." Thank you, Mr. President. "Yeah, I loved that blah, blah, blah." I meet George Bush at a big CEO's house in Georgia one day. I do not want to mention the name. There was a hundred people. He was my close friend. He invited me.

I meet George Bush two. He goes "Hi." Nice to meet you, Mr. President. Now at an America First event in Washington, DC, here I am thinking Donald Trump is going to say hello to me. Say hey man, thank you for your support, your articles, you know, blah blah blah blah. Whatever it is. Whole nine yards. They tell me on the line do not say anything to the president. You cannot talk to the President. So now you are muzzled. They told everybody. And I thought maybe they just said that for me. I do not know. So now you are on the line, and I meet him and that is all. That is it . . . Nobody told him.

Then later. Now two Democrats. Now I am an actor. Who am I going to vote for? If I am invisible to a party that I am supporting, at the end of the day. And that is the genius of the Democrats. They understand culture. Where the GOP is brain dead. And they resist culture because they think that the middle of America resents all of Hollywood. Which they do not. They do not resent all of us. That has to be fixed.

***

Davi—a straightforward Italian American—had to have the last say:

"If I had a chance to talk with him, I would tell him: We pray for you, Mr. President. It takes a lot of courage to do what you do here. Continue to do it and I know you are getting attacked on all sides. But continue to do what you do. And put people around you please that are going to give you the right information. Because you have a lot of people in this swamp even right in the White House that are not giving you the information you need.

Well, I would say that we continue to pray for you every day, Mr. President. For your safety, for your strength. Because what you are enduring is just an amazing thing. When you think about the attacks you get daily from inside and outside, and the fortitude you must have, the strength. Just pray and continue the course. Because you are doing the right thing for our nation. It is so important for our nation."

Kristy Swanson

Kristy was no different than any of the other conservatives in this group. She was outspoken. She displayed no fear or anxiety. She even rode with her husband and son all the way to Washington, DC, and stayed in the Willard with the filmmakers as their guest.

Being the only guests of this famous hotel when no one was venturing to the capital of the superpower, she was courageous, considering it was early days of the COVID-19 when everybody was yearning to remain isolated at home, not knowing if a hotel room was contagious.

> I am a patriot. I love my country. I was definitely supporting Trump, because what is not to like?
>
> —Kristy Swanson

Eerie Washington, DC, in March

Kristy Swanson is quite different in person from her heroic *Buffy the Vampire Slayer* image and her sometimes blunt political tweets.

During the two days we spent with her and her family in Washington, DC, she kept asking: "Why can't we all talk? Why can't we all get along?"

The logistics involved in filming with Kristy were not the usual ones. Far from it. While COVID-19 was taking over our normal life, Kristy, who resides in New Jersey with her husband, Lloyd Eisler, and their son, Magnus Hart Swanson Eisler, suggested they drive and meet us in DC.

"Safest way to travel," she concluded.

DC was dark and empty: No cabs, no open restaurants. The Willard Hotel, where we camped, had no room service. The gym was open per a guest (we were so few in house anyway). I worked out with triple masks, gloves, and threw my clothes into the laundry immediately.

It *was* a scary stay.

Yet, we managed to make the best socializing possible beside filming.

I threw a small (!) reception for Kristy, her husband, and her son in my hotel suite. Loretta Greene—whose is known in Washington's political and social scene—drove us to buy food and drinks.

Kristy asked us to include Mark Paoletta, a White House lawyer she had befriended, and arranged her visit at the Oval Office weeks prior.

We also included Trump loyalist Michael Caputo, who had been appointed as the mouthpiece for Health and Human Services (HHS) and would make headlines later for a Facebook meltdown.

Sean Spicer, whom Kristy supported loudly while he appeared on *Dancing with the Stars*, joined us later.

We spiced up the party with Michael Moussa-Adamo. Michael Moussa-Adamo, then was Gabon's ambassador to the US, now the defense minister of Gabon.

Keeping the COVID-19 rules, we still enjoyed the special evening.

It was one of these moments: "We were *there*."

Kristy Swanson: First Impression

When Daphne and Erbil first met Kristy at their large presidential suite in the Willard, opening the door to the dark hallway was a solemn affair. The lights turned brighter and then every time someone was coming or going. On that day, the hotel was practically empty.

Filming with "Buffy the Vampire Slayer"

The next day, Kristy came for the filming. She is pretty and let me know she had done her hair and makeup herself. . .Wow! Not common in Hollywood.

I started the interview by asking about her (and Dean Cain) visiting President Trump at the Oval Office, just when the pandemic was about to master our lives.

Kristy: I was here in DC for CPAC and I was doing a play with Dean Cain. It is called, *FBI Lovebirds: Undercovers*, and so we were invited to meet the president. It was exciting, and it was cool. He is very, very, very nice and we had a good visit. Just say hi and kind of chitty chat. It was very cool; it was an honor to meet him.

***

I reminded Kristy that it was interesting timing, because it was just the end of his [first] impeachment and the beginning of the COVID-19 pandemic. The headlines made fun of how the President found time to meet with Buffy and Superman.

Kristy: Yeah, there was some weird tweets about that. I do not understand why that would . . . Why that is a big deal, but I do not know it . . . Yeah, the first time that I've actually had a conversation with him and met him.

***

Visiting the Oval Office is a milestone for the ones privileged. I asked Kristy to reflect.

Kristy: So you could just talk to him and he talks to you and he's just a comfortable person to be around, and he's magnetic. He has just got this energy and that is just amazing, and I just loved his energy. He was exactly what I thought he would be.

Well, he made a joke to Dean. He said, "Next time you do the play, I'll be your understudy or something." He likes to cut up and make jokes and be funny, and he certainly is very funny. He has got a great sense of humor and so I do not know if there was . . . He did give us a couple of cool hats, some Trump hats, which was nice. It was just an honor to meet him.

Playing Lisa Page

Dean Cain and Kristy Swanson were in DC because of their play, *FBI Lovebirds*.

I asked Kristy about how she got involved in this unusual play. How did it come together? How did she and Dean, who is part of the *Trump vs. Hollywood* film as well, come to play the two lovebirds of the FBI?

Kristy: Well, it was Phelim McAleer and his wife Ann who took all the transcripts and the text messages of Lisa Page and Peter Strzok and put that all together to have it be like a verbatim, read-out loud, like a stage reading, and turn it into a play and they talked to Dean about it and they asked him if he would ask me if I would do the play.

I got a phone call from Dean and my jaw dropped. I go, "What? You want me to read on a stage?" I go, "I struggle already. I am dyslexic and I have a fear of a live audience. I am not used to that sort of form. I've never done a play." And I go, "I can't do this, Dean," and he goes, "No! You can do it." He is just such a cheerleader and he talked me into it, and the support of my family. I worked with a coach as well, just to get me familiar with the words.

My script was this thick because I had to have big words so that my eyes would track and I would not make any mistakes up on stage, so I had to put a lot of work into it. It was a big accomplishment for me, just from the fear factor of doing a play, and

I really liked it. I had a good time doing it. I am glad that Dean talked to me into it.

Actors often meet with true life story characters that they are portraying. Naturally, Trump- supporting Kristy had no access to his reported hater, Lisa Page.

Kristy: "Well, learning the character of Lisa was a little bit tough because there wasn't a whole lot out there to see specifically how she spoke or her mannerisms, at least not back then, last summer. That was a year ago. There is more out there now, she has done some interviews. The important part about it was. . . it is the script itself and the words and the things that were said. That was the most important thing to get across.

Yeah, normally I do a lot of character development and research and really get that character. . . I call it "in my belly" kind of thing, so I can really play it well. I think with them, when you read it, when you listen to it, it just exudes so much arrogance. They are texting back and forth and just the things that they said, it just exuded just a lot of arrogance, and that was really what we played up a lot was that kind of demeanor.

Political Involvement

Was she ever involved in politics before supporting Donald Trump?

Kristy: "I've not always been politically involved, but I'm interested in it and I'm a patriot. I love my country and so I think I have always paid attention, but I do not have a brain or a mind for it or anything. I am not highly educated in politics, but I am a mom, and I am a concerned citizen and I pay attention to things. I listen to things and I vote. Have I ever been vocal? Not really. I mean, I learned. . . I remember that I was going to vote for McCain, and I had said something in my social group in LA. I was with some girls and I had mentioned that I liked McCain and it was like, "Hiss." I got my eyes scratched out, like this whip around look like, "You're horrible to even think that way." So, I was like, "Oh okay, I shouldn't have brought that up; that was silly of me." But I do not know if I have been super political. I have just never really brought it up on set or at work, but I hear it all the time from others and just always kept quiet, I guess. And then I was definitely supporting Trump because what is not to like? He is for the most important thing: we, the people. That means everything to me.

When he was running, I started getting more out there about it. I just decided that life's too short. I spend forty years in a profession where I do not get to be myself, I am playing a character. So why can't I be myself in my own personal life?

Why is it not okay in Hollywood to be a conservative?

I just want to stand up for . . . I think it is okay to just be yourself. I have friends that vote Democrat, and we love each other. I have no problem with them, they have no problem with me, but then there are others that do tend to have a problem. I would never not work with someone because they did not think like me.

I feel that it is time to set the example of let us just all get along. We can learn from each other; we do not have to hate each other.

How do I explain it? I do not know if I could explain it. I feel like there has always been people over . . . whoever was president, there has always been haters and people that do not like. But this one is bad, I guess. I think because he is so upfront. So, he says what he thinks, he is not afraid to say it. And then maybe, I think they do not own him, they do not control him. That maybe is why they hate him; I do not know. They should just give him a chance. I think he is doing a really good job.

Blacklisting

I brought up the famous tweet by actress Debra Messing to blacklist donors who attended a Donald Trump fundraiser in Beverly Hills.

She looked saddened.

Kristy: Yes. I saw that tweet that she put out. I was like, "Wow, not even trying to hide it, that's wild."

Racist

The "R" question had to come up. "Is he (Trump) a racist?" Do not forget that George Floyd was yet to come.

Kristy: No, I don't think he's a racist. Not at all. I have even been called a racist on Twitter and stuff. I have been called all kinds of things. It is crazy.

I do not know if they want to upset you or . . . It's stupid.

Maybe I Lost Jobs? Maybe—I Gained!

Was Kristy blacklisted in Hollywood since she supported Trump?

Kristy: I can't prove it. I mean, sure, maybe, it is possible that I have not been considered for a job because I support the president. Who knows? But I cannot prove it and it is not worth the energy to think about or harp on it or anything like that. I do work. I make a living. I am a mom too, and life is fine. And I think after forty years, I mean, you do go through ups and downs in your career and where you are working quite a bit, depending on your age bracket and what is available and what is being written, you know what I mean? There is like, you always have peaks and valleys in your career anyway. And so, the last ten years I have spent, now that I have gotten older, I played the mom in a lot of Hallmark movies and Lifetime movies. And that is just where I have been and where I have fallen into, where I am supposed to be and wherever I am supposed to be is where I am supposed to be.

So, I do not like to ever feel like Hollywood decides who I am or what I am going to do, you know? It is like, I get to have choices too, you know. So, I cannot prove if I ever lost a job or was not considered because I am conservative. I have gotten a lot of jobs because I am conservative, maybe. I don't know.

He Did Not Need Hollywood

I was thinking out loud, that maybe Hollywood hated Trump, because they had been so used to being "needed" by political candidates?

Yeah, maybe. Maybe that is why. I do not know. I think it is awesome that he did not need Hollywood or the big glitz and glamor and all that stuff. But I have been disappointed in how Hollywood has reacted. It is sad because I think there is nothing wrong with a celebrity or star, whatever you want to call them, to have an opinion and want to support someone that is running for president or any office.

I think it is fine for someone like me, or someone like Dean Cain, or Whoopi [Goldberg]. Have your opinion. That is fine. I just do not think that it belongs at an award show on stage. I do not think it belongs on the red carpet at an event where we are celebrating.

Reality TV

Maybe, just maybe, Hollywood resented Trump for being just, a reality show star?

Kristy: Well, I mean times have changed, technology changes, shows change, ideas and all that stuff. What he did with his show was a great success. They loved it. How many seasons? It was a huge success, and America loved watching it. He shouldn't care.

No Celebrities in Trump Inauguration

Trump's team could not get the big names for his 2017 inauguration.

Seeing Lady Gaga, Jennifer Lopez, Tom Hanks, Jon Bon Jovi, and many others appearing at Joe Biden's 2021 inaugural big day, must have been a painful reminder.

Yet Kristy did not share the pain. She thought it worked best for Trump's massive base.

Kristy: "I liked it. I like how simple it is. It does not have to be all glitzy and glamour. I liked how simple it was. And I like how he has done a lot of things. Even when he had the football players over and they had burgers. I mean, that was awesome. They loved it. It is simple. I like that he has big ideas, and he gets things done. And everything with him is very big and powerful, but he is also very simple, and I think that people really relate to that."

Trump and the Media

I do not know. I mean, Trump is so smart. He has been dealing with the media his whole life. I remember, was it in the eighties, he is on the rag mags, dealing with the lies and scandals and stories and it is still happening. I like that he defends himself. I like that he defends his family. I like that he defends America.

He can defend himself; he defends his family, he defends us. Those are his morals. You are going to punch at me, I am going to have something to say about it.

I think he knows the media better than they know themselves.

And he knows his politics. He has studied it his whole life. He has always been interested in watching it and following it. And he is learned it his whole life, being around it. And he is on the right track. He said all the things that I remember saying in my early twenties. I remember thinking, "Why do we have our nose in so much business overseas when we really need help here?" We have homeless here. We have elders that need our help. He is all about the people and America first. And I have always felt that way since I came of voting age. And so, he speaks the same language I do.

Falling Out with Friends Over Trump

Some families faced falling outs or lost friendships over supporting or opposing Donald Trump.

Kristy: I've had a few, I guess. They are not popping in my brain right now because I do not dwell on it. It is never like, "Oh yeah, I remember that time." Yeah. I mean, I have been attacked on Twitter and stuff and I have had a couple disagreements, but I never let it get like super ugly, you know?

Yeah. I mean, I can tell you Tom Arnold came after me, but I am not the only one he has come after. I am not special.

I am not special in that regard. I mean, he has gone after Dean. He is. . . that is his thing, so. . . But Jon Voight is the loveliest person. I have known him for years. James Woods. He is amazing.

Yeah, but maybe he does not want to work. Maybe he does not have to. Maybe he does not feel like it. Maybe he has done acting, you know what I mean?

I do not think it is because. . . It is funny, people they make these judgements, they call you like. . . I think it was, "You're A-lister. Now you're B-listed." Now it is, "No, you're on the D-list." And now it is the Z-list. You know, it is always changing.

It is crazy. But you know, it does not. . . I do not cry about it, you know. And I have seen people call James Woods, one of the greatest actors, a Z-lister, you know? "Oh, he doesn't even work." You know that kind of stuff they say. And it is like, "Well maybe he doesn't want to, maybe he doesn't have to." You do not know his life. You do not know him. And maybe he is quite happy just playing cards. He likes to play cards; poker and you know.

Do you see, if he is reelected in November 2020, do you think there is any way to repair this relationship or do you think it will just stay there until the end of his presidency?

How would I? I would not know what to do other than just. . . It is sad. I just, I wish that people would. . . I mean, I did not vote for Obama and I was not a huge fan of him, but I did not internally hate him. You know what I mean? It was not like that. I still supported the president.

"I Love Trump"

Can I give you a hug? No, shake my hand, whatever. But just, I love him. I just love him. He is so awesome. His energy's amazing. And I wish everybody could understand that he comes from such a good place. He has got our best interest at heart, and I wish they would stop treating him like he is the enemy because he is not.

Well, maybe he is an enemy of several people, like Lisa Page and others who. . . Because he decided to stop it. To stop what they were doing. So maybe he is their enemy. And in their mind, he is an enemy.

Robert De Niro

Robert De Niro. Yeah. He is a great actor, and I would just. . . I'd say, "Come on, do you really have to go on stage and do that? It doesn't look good." Nothing wrong with you if you do not like the guy, okay. But do you have to go on stage and say "F the president," come on.

I would be honest with him. I have never met him, but I would have no problem saying. . . I would not say do not have your feelings. You can have your feelings, but just do not do what you did.

Golf with Trump

I guess if Trump were sitting here right now, I would say, "Can I play a round of golf with you?" I would love to go golfing with Trump. That would be fun. I am consistently inconsistent. We all have bad days in golf, but some days I am great.

The Show Must Go On

Mark Geragos and Avi Lerner were continuing their business uninterrupted. In fact, under certain conditions they were doing excellent. Mark was going to his office in Los Angeles and representing more cases. Avi was flying from Dominican Republic to Bulgaria and continued filming.

Mark Geragos

Mark was objective and observant. He knew the issues involving President Trump well and what was transpiring politically in America during these challenging times.

> No, Donald Trump did not come up the way of a traditional
> Republican using the party, he remade the party.
>
> —Mark Geragos

Not a Pleasant Place to Go: Downtown Los Angeles

Mark Geragos has an office in downtown Los Angeles. He has his own building, and even had a courtroom in there.

They filmed the interview there but going to downtown Los Angeles was a difficult process. Nothing was open. Where to park the car was an issue.

Walking a block or two was also difficult. One had to be careful, as many homeless and beggars were loitering on the streets.

***

In 2020, in America, downtown Los Angeles was not unique with this scene. Erbil had gone out of his hotel room in Washington just to get a feeling of the city in their first visit after COVID-19. Daphne was horrified until he got back.

Erbil then had described that he walked two blocks and back and counted eight homeless people. He described them as old and young, educated, desperate, different ethnicity and race. Everyone in America was represented.

***

Daphne and Erbil stopped going to New York after October 2020. First, the city was officially shut—closed. Second, New York was not a "friendly" city in the first place.

Now with harsher conditions coupled with COVID-19 and winter, there was no reason to venture there.

Los Angeles has been known to have nearly a hundred thousand homeless before COVID-19. It was a disaster waiting to turn into a worse plague right out of the Middle Ages.

Then COVID-19 came in full force and further decimated the city. Their filming with Mark was in the summertime, before everything became worse.

Big Stars, Big Cases, Big City Los Angeles, Big Problems

Mark Geragos has represented some of Hollywood's biggest stars when they got in trouble. Chris Brown, Kesha, Puff Daddy, Winona Ryder, and Colin Kaepernick are only few of them. In fact, Mark and I became friends when I was interviewing Michael Jackson and his parents, and he represented Michael. He was later fired by Jackson. Jackson famously said: "It is my butt here."

Geragos and I stayed friends, even though Bill is Turkish-American and Gregos is Armenian-American. In addition, Gregos is suing the Turkish government, on behalf of the Armenian community.

Mark is flamboyant, fun, and full of historical knowledge. And no! He cannot stand Donald Trump!

The fact that he represented Colin Kaepernick after the latter knelt down during the playing of the national anthem and drove Trump into a flood of angry tweets probably added fuel to the fire.

Maybe Donald Trump was manipulating this fuel to energize his base?

Mark would have intelligent answers to many of my questions.

Whether one is a liberal or right wing, Mark Geragos is an entertaining interviewee who has had a front-row seat to recent history.

We met at his downtown office in LA. Geragos had his own private courtroom inside the building. Sounds grand? Not if you met Geragos.

Mark Geragos: One of the beautiful things about America is that you can vote with your pocketbooks, so to speak, or you can vote with boycotting somebody's products. And it has actually had an effect.

Right. But ironically, look at who one of Trump's early. . . I do not want to call him necessarily a mentor, but attached [was] Roy Cohn. Cohn, during the McCarthy hearings, was the counsel to Joseph McCarthy. And that is where the blacklisting actually ended up starting. So, there is a certain amount of irony here. Also, at the same time, the president was a part of Hollywood. He was on TV for, I think, fourteen seasons. He had a highly rated juggernaut. He was affiliated with Mark Burnett, who is one of the most powerful people in Hollywood. And by the way, the *Access Hollywood* tape shows you there's probably God knows how much material that is on the cutting room floor from all the time that he spent in Hollywood. And clearly somebody who is very attuned in the ratings.

Blacklisting

Well, look, I have had the situation, especially more recently in the #MeToo era, where certain clients of mine have either lost or not gotten deals because of their history or because all of a sudden, we're in the crosshairs. So, I understand that I have been in a position where I have defended people who I thought were unfairly targeted. Most recently Jussie Smollett, I think even though the case was dismissed and refiled at the time, it took a lot of courage for people to still employ him, given all of the kinds of the machinations that surrounded his case. So, it cuts both ways. And now you are finding that especially in the #MeToo movement, that it is a real problem for the blowback with Joe Biden.

So, there is an interesting dynamic that goes back and forth. Which leads me to one of the ironies of this administration. Finally, there are people who are saying, wait a second here coming out of the cavern here, coming out of other things. Due process is all of a sudden, is getting a second look, but it's not getting a second look by the people who have traditionally been proponents of due process. Traditionally as a left-wing, progressive Democrat, I will tell you that was something that I always embraced and thought of as kind of one of the pillars of the Democratic Party. Now we have gotten into a situation where the Republican Party has all of a sudden taken up the mantle of the due process.

The idea of fairness, just within the last weeks as we are filming this there has been a controversy because under Title IX, Betsy DeVos, who was not exactly a left-wing liberal, who was the secretary, I believe, of education has started to try to tinker with the presumptions under Title IX that ironically, thirty years ago, thirty-five years ago, that would have been a Democratic, progressive liberal position? No longer, which just proves a point: I have always said a Democrat is a Republican [that] has been indicted until you are facing the full force credit of the United

States government. Whether it is in the DOJ, the SEC, the IRS, you do not quite understand how important the presumption of innocence, due process, and those things are.

Why Hollywood Reacts So Bad When Trump Announced?

Well, take a look at who hired him and put him on the air back in 2003, 2004, Jeff Zucker. Who was then working for NBC, who apparently was instrumental in *The Apprentice* being put on the air? Jeff Zucker's new job is head of CNN. And CNN, if you listen to Donald Trump or you watch it, is kind of the opposition voice or the voice of the resistance. NBC, where he used to be, or Trump used to be where he made a lot of money for them now, has MSNBC and MSNBC is virtually from dawn to sundown an anti-Trump vehicle. And it is holding him accountable if you will. So, politics makes strange bedfellows is the only expression.

I mean, I was thinking with a friend of ours it is very suspicious . . . CBS, he was very close to him and her. I am not going to say it, but she is far off against Donald Trump. You would figure it yourself or she came up with this idea maybe Hollywood is personal, very emotional.

It Was the Same with Bill Clinton—I Was There

It is clearly, but people tend to forget, one of the pivotal points in my career was representing Susan McDougal. A lot of people do not even remember who Susan McDougal is. But back in the nineties, Susan McDougal was subpoenaed to go testify in front of the Whitewater grand jury. She refused; she was held in contempt. The independent counsel when I got involved was none other than our Ken Starr. Starr was coming after Susan McDougal. Susan was not going to sing from the script that the independent counsel wanted her to. And she complained bitterly about the US government and what the US government is doing. And frankly, when we went to trial, she was acquitted. I am not guilty of twelve counts here in Los Angeles, but then we went and tried to race in Arkansas, right? Smack dab in the middle of Bill Clinton's impeachment. And she was acquitted, found not guilty of obstruction of justice. Actually, one of the old-way obstruction of justice trials that has ever been done by an independent counsel has been found not guilty and that was Susan. Everything that Susan said at the time, everything that President Clinton was saying, at the time, in real time, it is almost as if you had taken the same playbook and its exactly what Trump is now, President Trump has done arguing. So, there is a certain amount of irony given the twenty years of what has happened.

And so, people can talk about how politicized it is now, but it was just as politicized in reverse twenty years ago. I had a front-row seat to it, I saw it. In fact, one of the things that I found ironic at the time back in 1998 was when we selected that jury for Susan, we had seven Democrats and five Republicans on the jury. She was acquitted, found not guilty on the obstruction of justice on the criminal contempt. Which you know, most people would say is a slam dunk for the prosecution. It was a hung jury, guess what the split was? Seven to five. Yeah. So, the country down to the jurors were split right down the middle twenty years ago. Just this, we have not made a lot of progress twenty years, twenty-two years later.

No, Donald Trump did not come up the way of a traditional Republican using the party, he remade the party. And Hillary Clinton who won the popular vote did come up the traditional way that somebody does to the Democratic Party. And there were a lot of people who were also heavily invested in the candidacy of Hillary Clinton. And it became the same kind of a fight. The only issue, I would take issue with this idea that it was not as polarized because I remember living through Whitewater. I remember living through Richard Mellon Scaife, and the *American Spectator* and David Bossie. All those guys were around, but on the other side, as anti-Clinton. They have grown up, made a lot more money. And they now are the Trump defenders. They were the Clinton attackers. So, I have had a front-row seat to it. I see it more in stark political terms. And I also think, Hollywood was in love with Bill Clinton. And he had a great base in Hollywood, and that is not true of Donald Trump.

I think it is personally because there are issues that people care about in Hollywood and he is on the opposite side of most of those issues. These are people who are heavily invested in choice. There are people who are heavily invested in immigration. I could go through all the tipped off various social issues. The one thing you have to give Trump credit for is he knows. . . Very similar to Karl Rove, who was George W. Bush's kind of strategist. Karl Rove used to say, "I know how to rile them up." He used to say, "Rile up to the crazies," but he said, "I know how to rile them up." Whether that was Hillary, it was him segregating with Hillary talking about the deplorables.

There is the use of social issues to fire up the base, even though some observers, myself included, feel like you rile them up with the social issues and they end up making bad choices for themselves economically. But if you understand the kind of dynamic—and there is a long arc of history. Whether it is the South, whether it is remnants of the Civil War, whether it is remnants of institutional or structural racism, there were just more things at work here.

Trump's Comeback

I always thought that his comeback from the rise and fall was something that was admirable at the time, financially. People talk about, his father bailed him out, his father did this or that, but there is a certain admirable quality of the way that he understands self-promotion. How we use the self-promotion, how he came back from. . . It is very few people who have had billions, lost it all and been negative, and then made a comeback from it and remade themselves. He has remade himself on a couple of occasions and that is a tough thing to do, so you have to admire that.

At the same time, my day job is as a criminal defense lawyer, even though my practice is now primarily civil. But the things he talks about in criminal justice and the things that are happening in the criminal justice system are traditionally what we on the defense bar had been screaming about for forty years. And now it is interesting, especially in light of what's happened with Michael Flynn, especially what's happened with the kind of attorney of the tables, the DOJ cannibalizing itself. It is just an interesting time to be living, to watch the pendulum swing.

Colin Kaepernick

I will never forget doing the Jerry Jones [Dallas Cowboys owner] deposition, which was later leaked, I did not really get, but it was leaked. And Jerry Jones candidly admitted that Donald Trump had apparently told him, if you believe what was leaked, that in fact Trump said, "This is a winning issue for me, get out of my way." Because remember at the very beginning, Jerry Jones kneeled down with his players in solidarity, got a phone call from Trump and that ended that. Then it was if you kneel as a Cowboy [player] you are done. So, he hijacked that issue, with Colin Kaepernick, he took Colin to task. And if you read the Mueller Report and I know that is also a touchstone for people to go crazy, but if you read the Mueller Report, there is documented evidence, apparently, that the Russians embraced and decided to kind of [emit] chaos surrounding Colin Kaepernick.

There was a certain degree of irony now with the stay-at-home orders. I have been on both sides of that issue as well. But people who are now protesting to stay-at-home orders are the same people who were saying he was inappropriate for Colin and Eric [Reid] to be kneeling on the football field. Well, I find that ironic because there is an argument that health wise and medical wise you're endangering people by getting out there and protesting in violation of the stay-at-home order. At the same time, you were saying Colin Kaepernick and Eric Reid had no right or Kenny Stills to kneel during the national anthem. So, it is a physical act, protest, on both sides, but it depends on whose ox is getting gored.

And I wanted to advocate on that because some of the actors that we have already interviewed, some of the ones that actually support Donald Trump, some are declining. Some are scared to decline it. And one woman declined it and complained that they cannot get a job in Hollywood or was ever like that. And actually, also the other side I've been getting as a Republican and Donald's friend and Donald's delegate, all kinds of jokes, at last Colin Kaepernick got a job. You know what I am saying? So basically, he could not get a job properly either. So . . .

There is a certain degree of irony to find people who are complaining about the fact that they support Trump and cannot get a job, are the same people who are supportive of the fact that the NFL will not hire Colin Kaepernick. So, given that the irony is it comes back to the same situation. It just depends. . . Your political beliefs tend to drive how you view this situation as opposed to rational thinking.

You are just bringing me to one, maybe a question, Mark. Basically, do you feel like maybe Donald Trump, and by the way, he wants to beat up, nobody likes to be rejected. You know, from time to time privately would say, does he express a very like me? And you know, he is very demanding, but do you think because he is such a smart strategist, that is how we won the elections, do you think he sometimes in graces the hatred of Hollywood because he thinks he is good for his base?

I think that without question, I think when you are having seen and heard him say, "This is a winning issue for me involving Colin Kaepernick." That is somebody who has got enough self-awareness to know when you make the other works, this is a winning issue. You understand intellectually that if you hijack that message and say, "Get that son of a bitch off the field." Or would not you just love the ownership to do that. It is a twofer for him, he is firing up his base, he is embracing the patriotism. And at the same time, by the way, which famously has been called the last refuge of the scoundrel. But at the same time, it is somebody who has got enough self-awareness to do what Karl Rove used to tell George W. Bush would rile up the crazies. Anytime you have got some kind of a situation that you want to deflect from, how you do that? You go to somewhere else. He is a smart enough guy to understand that.

This is a guy who took major international banks to the woodshed and got them to give him more money after he had squandered great sums.

For people who say this guy is a moron, or he does not understand anything. He is a warrior, he is crafty, and he is smart like a fox.

This is somebody who has somehow survived through all kinds of machinations and all kinds of losses that would have floored an ordinary person and he succeeded. So, you have to have some kind of understanding that he gets or understands what he's doing. And sometimes, I think what the left does not understand, is they feed into that and they feed into it exactly the way he wants them to.

Daphne: So, if he were standing in front of you, Donald Trump, what would you tell him?

Mark: I would tell him you probably, I know that this has been successful, this method has been successful for you. And I know that you probably feel like do not tamper with the success, but the collateral damage that it causes for you to win in this way is not worth it from a legacy standpoint. From a legacy standpoint, most people want to be loved, most people do not want to be hated. And from a legacy standpoint, you could have brought people together. There are opportunities to bring people together. And I do not know why you consistently run away from that. I understand that you have always won by virtue of your characterization of winning. But at some point, you are taking the short way, at some point, you have got to take a longer view.

Would I Meet Trump?!

I have met him before. Look, one of the things that frustrates me sometimes with the judicial system is you can do battles inside of a courtroom. It is ironic that we are sitting in here court, but ideology has infected the courtroom, just like it as everywhere else in America. That ideology affected the courtroom thirty, forty, more a hundred years ago. But it never kind of seeped out as much into society as we see[#] it on display now. One of the things I have always said is that you could not do battle in the courtroom and then go outside the courtroom and have a drink or share a meal or something else because you are on ideological other sides. So, I do not have that problem.

Avi Lerner

The name Avi Lerner may not ring an immediate bell to people outside Hollywood, but inside— he is a mega film producer. He has done more than four hundred movies with such A-listers as Robert De Niro, Al Pacino, and Morgan Freeman.

And of course, he and Sylvester Stallone are behind the hit *Expendables*.

Avi Lerner—an Israeli American—supported Hillary Clinton against Donald Trump in 2016. He joined another powerful Israeli American, Haim Saban, who hosted fundraisers at his home for the Democratic candidate.

So, I expected him, to go on an anti-Trump Hollywood rant.

Well. . . I would be surprised . . . He had some criticism, but it came in a loving manner, mixed with actual compliments.

I Do Not Like Hollywood

The busy producer has love-hate relations with what Hollywood represents.

Avi Lerner: I am very passionate about making movies. . . Except that I don't like to be associated with Hollywood because I personally don't like Hollywood people. I do not like the way they approach the business. When I say Hollywood people, to me it is those people that have got their own society, they are breaking, they have got their own idea about politics, about approaching, about what kind of movie you like to do.

And if you do not do their movie, you are out of it. I am trying to stay out of Hollywood, but using the idea of making movies because I do passionately. . . I do like to make movies. That is what I have been doing all my life. Started when I finished the Israeli army and then did over four hundred movies and I am very proud of it.

We did *The Expendables*, we did *The Hitman's Bodyguard*, *The Angel Has Fallen*. There's *Hell Boy* and so on, and so on. *Rambo*, it's an old movie that has got the franchise and we do it again and again and again.

***

Talking about Hollywood and politics is not Avi's favorite topic, but when I pushed him, he was bluntly honest.

Donald, Arnold, and China . . .

Avi: I'm not familiar very much because as I said, I wasn't born here. I was not associated in Hollywood and Los Angeles. But I can tell you that yes, you are right. Hollywood people and mainly very liberal Democrats in a way, that they hate anything to do with a Republican, anything to do with in this case, with Donald Trump. It was not like this because Ronald Reagan, although he was a Republican, came from Hollywood. So, they liked it, then it was this."

Daphne: I reminded Avi that he worked with the epitome of "Hollywood meets politics"—Arnold Schwarzenegger.

Avi: I love Arnold and Arnold is a Republican, but even Arnold doesn't like Donald Trump. I think Donald has got . . . And we met him. I met him before he became a president. Donald is a very, very smart man in his own way. He knows how to drive what he needs. He believes that what he is doing, is good for the country.

He is very, I must say, very patriotic, very cared about America. It is all about Americans and America, America, bigger gain or whatever he said. On the other hand, I think Donald is sometimes his own worst enemy. For an example, he wants to create . . . And for me, this is the one thing that I disagree with him regarding China.

For some reason, the Republicans and Donald believe that China is responsible for the pandemic. Yes, it came from China and maybe China did not tell us when it happened and maybe they covered the news. But I do not believe they did it on purpose. There was no reason for them to do it. There is no gain for them.

Also, I want to say on the same talking point that I want to do something in China and build the relationship in China. However, Chinese are very difficult businesspeople. For example, we know that when you do business with the Chinese, you only start to negotiate after you have signed the contract. That is a fact.

On the other hand, we need China from our point of view, to sell the movies. Number one decide America.

For the movie business. . . I do not care about the rest. I care about the movie business and if they do not buy our movie, we are in trouble. So, I wish there were a way that Donald Trump did not fight with President Xi . . .That we can go back to business like we used to sell. We used to sell a lot of movies to China, so that is my critiques about that.

They do not want to buy any movie from us anymore. At least they are independent. The whole Chinese system of the propaganda, which is wrong, but we have to deal with it. The relationship between Donald Trump and President Xi caused it. 100 percent! It stopped there.

I think to our business, the film business, it is very important to find a way to be able to sell our movie to China and get their price because without it, we are all in trouble. That's my personal thing.

Stop the Piracy

Another area that the veteran producer finds, where Hollywood needs Washington DC is regarding piracy.

Avi: Yeah. Well, this is the most important thing for me besides the other problem that we are facing, the movie business, that I do not think the politician is doing nothing that's piracy. They do not give a shit about people, copyright and those kinds of things.

They said they will, they have, but they do not do anything. When you have got a company like Google and Facebook, and they are stealing our movie and nobody does anything about it, it makes me sick. Or all the telephone companies, the big telephone companies, they are stealing our movie.

And when I say stealing, they do not help to stop this. I do not know, when I see somebody steal a car in the street, I will go and try to stop it. When all the telephone companies see and can stop stealing our movie in piracy, our movie, they say, "Oh, they've got no rights to do this," standing behind them. And I do not understand. This is the second problem that I have got. China and the piracy situation.

Blacklisting / Two Countries

Avi's reaction time to "blacklisting" was fast. He was neither shocked nor "politically correct." Yes, he has been concerned about our growing division.

Avi: Number one, everyone knows the political view of most of the people. Most of the smart actors stay out of this. You take for an example, an actor that I admire, Morgan Freeman. He is out of the politics thing. So obviously he has got his own view about the politics, but there is a lot, a lot, a lot, and that is not mainly on the movie business, but it is all over what is happening today in the country.

I feel like we are building two countries. Two completely different countries. One is California and New York, and then one is in the middle that it is different. It is very sad what is happening. And the main reason, the main reason is those people that do not let you talk.

And God forbid you say your opinion. I will give you an example from my personal view. There is a good director called Bryan Singer. He has been blamed for molesting children thirty years ago. There was never proof about it, but there's always rumors about it and when I was going to hire him to do one of my movies, I said, "Listen, what I learned about the law is you are only proven guilty when you're guilty. You don't blame people just because of the Twitter role or just because somebody thinks so."

And I had been affected so badly by the internet, by people who say to me, "How dare you protect Bryan Singer?" I said, "I don't believe he's done it." But who am I to fight with the millions of people?

So I didn't have a choice. I had to fire him or do not carry on making the movie with him, but it is hurting me. And it does not stop there, when you say things, and I do not want to sound terrible. I do not agree what happened when a policeman can kill and really murder somebody [George Floyd].

But on the other hand, it is not everyone. You do not have to kill all the policemen. You need them. We need them to protect us. And all this liberal people that say, "Get rid of them," they will suffer when somebody attacks their home. They'll suffer.

***

I pushed again about blacklisting, bringing up Debra Messing's tweet to blacklist Trump supporters.

Horrible, horrible things to even think about. As I said before in this conversation, we should be open to listening what the other side says. We should not blacklist like what happened today with Facebook. It is scary. Half of the country is not going to blacklist.

Is Trump Racist? No! Stupid?

Avi is so straightforward that he agreed with me: "If someone is accused of being racist today? In Hollywood, it's dead. . . It is over."

And Donald Trump: Is he a racist?

Avi: No. 100 percent no. I will give you the simple example. His daughter is Jewish. He cannot hate his daughter. And by the way here, I do not want to get into trouble with Donald Trump, but his favorite daughter. And her husband is Jewish.

And I like Donald Trump mainly for one reason, and only one reason. He is the biggest supporter of Israel. I am an Israeli.

I like my country. I do not agree with a lot of the things that happen in my country. But I like the fact that Donald Trump supports Israel all the way, in every place there. I do not know what you call racist.

I do not know. Definitely he is not against black people because he has got some of the people in his cabinet or working with him like the doctor, Ben Carson.

He's definitely not racist, not by nature. By the way, he grew up in New York where New York is a lot left and right, and it is all together. Donald Trump is not racist. Donald Trump says sometimes things that nobody else will say and I do not want to even use the word, but it is so stupid that it seems like lies.

Like he said, "All the people voted, and Hillary Clinton won the popular [vote] by four million people." Why? And because of the system that is in America and it is the existing system, and he became the president of the United States, but he did not win the popular. And he said that all these people came from [the] cemetery and this. It is not necessary to say it. It is stupid of him to say it.

Or the biggest inauguration ever. . .And even recently when he went to Oklahoma, we saw that it was a lot of empty seats. . . Look again, I am not here to defend him, and I am definitely not here to blame him. I think he cares about the country, there is no question in my mind. And he can do a lot of the things in a different way, but that is the kind of president we chose. And we need to respect it.

I Voted for Hillary

I supported Hillary, I donated money for her. I still like her. By the way, I voted for her against Trump, but that is what happened. You lost, now Donald Trump is the [president]. I do not think the tactic that he used against her was right, but he won. That is the system.

Casting Black

For Avi, his casting of minorities is not because it is fashionable. It comes naturally and has commercial reasons as well.

Avi: Look, the truth when I make movies, I always look. . . If you look at *The Expendables*, two of the guys actually were black.

I mean, most of the movies that I do, I look at Mexican, European. I look into natural, I look at this as total importance for one reason and only one reason, to sell the movie. So, I think it is very important to have black people and white people, and Mexican people, and Jewish people and whatever to put in the movie, because it makes us one nation.

What is happening today on both sides, it makes me sick. For an example, when you say something that the liberal Democrats do not agree, you are dead. They ban you; they are attacking you. Why? Everyone should be entitled to say whatever he believes, and you do not have to agree. And you do not have to fight.

You have to say, "Let's agree to disagree." And by the way, at the end of the day, we all agree the same thing: Life is more important than many things that they put in. . . The value of life.

I have studios all over the world. I have got studios in England, I have got studios in Greece, I am building one, I have got studios in Portugal. I am building now one in Dominican Republic . . . So, I have got studios all over the world and I make movies all over the world. I may prefer to work there. I don't like this system, the idea of fear of saying things, even if you say something.

I Was There When De Niro Attacked Arnold

I was with Arnold in a fundraiser for the Israeli army and I was embarrassed for Robert De Niro. I like Robert De Niro. I made a movie with him. I do not agree with him on a lot of things. . . I think he is a very nice person.

He is a nice person.

But when he attacked Arnold Schwarzenegger, accusing him of supporting Donald Trump? Number one, Arnold

Schwarzenegger has the right to support whoever he wants. But more important, Arnold Schwarzenegger did not support Donald Trump and the way it went on, we had to make De Niro relax, and I do like De Niro. In any case, I do not agree with his political idea, but I do like him, and he has got the right to express . . . Him and Al Pacino are great to work with.

Most of the people, most of the actors that I am working, are Democrats. Fine. I respect them. I like it. But do not have to agree with them. I believe in capitalism. I do not like socialism. I do not like communism. I do not like the union.

The only thing they have got is Tom Cruise and Robert De Niro and Brad Pitt, they need the union to protect them. They have got more money than the union. So, it is a funny thing and because of those people, they need the union.

But one day, somebody will wake up and say, "Enough is enough. You cannot torture these people." Look what happened even in the Obama time in Detroit, Michigan. They had to stop making cars because of the union.

They do not realize it, but the reason why we are losing so much work to overseas, not because of the people. The work in America is by far better than anywhere else, but the union, the money they are taking away, those things, it is impossible to live like this. They have to wake up!

CHAPTER FIVE

Cancel Culture and No-No Rhetoric

Cancel culture and No-No rhetoric are terminologies that came to life with the Trump presidency. They are brought up by the liberals against the conservatives.

Before that, there was "politically correct" in place. It was replaced with these two. Changing times!

Focusing on Trump's persona and ignoring idiosyncrasies of Hollywood were now determining the fate of Americans.

Trump Persona

From the conservative perspective, nothing that President Trump would say or do was going to be right from the perspective of the liberals. Cancel culture and No-No rhetoric were the proof in the pudding.

Liberals would go further and call the Trump Presidency "lunacy" while the conservatives would point to the "wisdom" of the forty-fifth president.

Claudia Jordan, as a former personal friend of Donald Trump, would pose the question during the interview: "Donald, what happened to you?"

Dean Cain, on the other hand, would frankly say: "President Trump will get criticized no matter what he does."

All the while, Isaiah Washington was the only African American on the conservative side who came out defending Trump and going after Hollywood with vengeance.

Lunacy: Claudia Jordan

Eric Roberts used the word "lunatic" during his interview. That was the most incendiary comment from the liberal corner.

Yet, Claudia Jordan had plenty to say about Donald J. Trump, who she knew for a long time as a close personal friend, and posed the question to emphasize her very point: "Donald, what happened to you?"

Claudia Jordan is not a friend of Donald Trump. She used to be. She describes a cheeky, sort of flirty at times, friendship that finished, "when he attacked Barack Obama."

Claudia's opinions are common among many African Americans. Rapper Eric B would tell me: "I am glad you included Claudia. She is my girl. She speaks her mind."

Yes, she did. The Trump issues are also personal to her, "Because we used to be friends. *What?!* Did he lie to me [about who he is] all this time?"

I noticed that Claudia got along with another of the film's interviewees, conservative host Bill Whittle. He was scheduled to be interviewed by me at the same day, so Bill introduced everyone and hosted dinner after the filming.

Though Whittle is all the way to the right of Claudia, it was social, cordial.

Bill Whittle was nice.

Claudia was polite.

But not when the conversation turned to Donald Trump: it is too personal, too close to her heart.

Claudia Jordan: It is very polarizing right now . . . America is terrible right now. Let me talk about my background, and who I am, what I am. My mother is from Italy. She is an Italian immigrant in the United States. My father is a black, former member of the Air Force. To me there has always been two Americas.

People like me have always felt the division. I think now, more people are feeling what a lot of us have been feeling for a very long time. I grew up, from an early age being told I had to pick a side. Are you black, are you white? What are you? Then when I became—I started working more, and when you become a little more successful, it is the haves and the have nots. But I really feel like now the rest of the country is saying what it feels like. It is awful.

I felt like every single day something could happen in my life. I grew up afraid of police. I feel like we see the same country two totally different ways right now. And for some people they are happy, they love it. And for some people they hate it, and they are fearful every single day. And that is sad, because this is supposed to be the best country in the world, and right now we are not living up to that. We are not.

My Friendship with Trump

Claudia first met with Trump when she was a beauty queen, and then she was cast twice on *The Apprentice*.

Claudia: The first time I met Donald Trump, I teased him after because I do not think he remembers. It was 1997, he had just purchased the Miss USA Pageant. That year I competed, I [as] Miss Rhode Island. And we met, it was quick, we did not keep in touch. Nothing like that. And then years later I was a model on *Deal or No Deal*, on NBC, and *Celebrity Apprentice* came on after our show. So, they came to our show to promote *Apprentice*. While he is on set, he is kind of flirting with some of the girls, talking to some of the girls. It was not bad, but he was just feeling people out as far as, I want to put a model on next season. I was into real estate, so he comes up to me and he says, "I heard you're the girl that I need to talk to, because everyone said talk to Claudia." He comes up to me, I say, "It's about damn time you came up to me. Yes, I am the one who needs to be on your show.

So he liked how feisty I was. And very opinionated, I never back down with him. And I also feel like he respects me pretty much because I was not just a yes woman, agreeing with everything he said. And that is when we became friends. He started to call me. I am not going to lie, he did flirt with me at first, and I think he tried to shoot his shot a little bit. But I am definitely not going to be anyone's mistress. And immediately he started to respect me as his friend. He will call me. I would call him sometimes in a meeting and I am like, do not pick up the phone in a meeting, people are going to think this is more than it is. And then once he got it in his mind that he wanted to put me on the show, no one could tell him otherwise. So, then he fought for me.

***

What made Claudia feel so good about her friendship with Donald Trump, was the way he treated her like a close friend.

Claudia: What intrigued me about him was, he was very outspoken, and he was accessible. Meaning, you are a billionaire, but you still were of the people, is what I thought. You know what I mean, he did not have this air about himself, like he was untouchable. So, the fact that he was personable, and we would talk, he would give me advice on things, and vice versa. We talked about politics, we talked about Barack Obama, we talked about John McCain. I told him he was crazy to support Sarah Palin as a vice president because I think she is an idiot. And so, he liked it. I enjoyed our conversations.

I remember one time being in his office and he had a camera crew that was not some really huge production, and they were all African American, and he let them come in and interview him. And I thought that was really good because a lot of times in the beginning of your career it is hard to get those big interviews. I like that about him. So, it sucks to me how things have changed as far as my perception of him as a man. But I really liked how he moved. And he is a success story. He was in rappers' songs, pop culture loved Donald Trump at one point. He has a lot of celebrity friends, black friends.

The Barack Obama Factor

I think I can speak for myself and the people that I know. I think a lot of us feel betrayed. We feel like, you are not that same person that I saw let this young black camera crew come into your office. You are not that same person that will call and check up on me. You are not that same person that would say these things that you say, that offends us. I want to just make this very clear, when it comes to Black America, and Barack Obama, even if you do not agree with his policies, the fact that the first African American president was elected is very special to us. And for someone to just be so hard against it, and to diminish everything he has ever done and said, we take it personally.

And that is when our friendship fell apart, because imagine, and you are not from America as well, imagine seeing a president of your nationality for the very first time in a country that always had the same exact framework. The same exact model, an older white man. And then you would see someone from your country. Just like if an Italian president were elected, everyone that was Italian American would be so excited.

So all of us that had Donald Trump's back and loved him, to see the way he really went after Barack Obama, it really hurt. It hurt because, say you do not like that man's policy, but do not accuse him of being basically a liar, and not really being an American citizen. And what that does for black people, when you ask to see their paperwork, and to prove who they are, it is all too close to what the slave masters used to do to freshly, newly released slaves. Show me your papers, boy. And that is what it felt like, and that is a huge slap in the face. I was a fan of Donald Trump, I was a friend of Donald Trump, I have his phone number in my phone to this day. I do not know if he changed it or not, but if he did not, I still have the old Blackberry phone number. At first, I did not say anything negative about him publicly, because I remember what he did for me and how he fought for me. But then he just kept on going, and kept on going, and I felt like he abandoned the friends that he had that were black, and African American, and of color that really vouched for him.

Trump Told Me, "McCain is My Friend"

Claudia recalls the one time she discussed Obama with Trump. He told her he had to support his friend. . .yes, John McCain.

Claudia: I had one conversation with him in his office. Me and my friend Kelly went to the office, because when I was in New York I would go by and say, hey I am in town, want to come by and say hello. So, I remember he had a picture of Sarah Palin photoshopped with a porn star's boobs, so it was boobs were out with Sarah Palin's face. And I said, "I know you're not going to support them." And he says, "Well I like your guy." Meaning Barack Obama. "But it's just that John McCain is my friend, and I feel like I have to support him." But he had nothing negative to say about Barack Obama, he did not say he was not an American citizen, he did not say he is a Muslim and all these other things.

So, for it to change, I was like. . . I feel like the country would have embraced him so much more if you kind of respect the one that came before you. Because I am sure Donald Trump would like the next president that comes after him to kind of include him in some things. Like, hey, how did you handle this crisis, or can I get some advice. It is just disrespectful. And the world does not revolve around Donald Trump, and I feel like he had everything in his reach to be a really good president. Because on some things he does, some of his policies have been very beneficial, especially for the people that have money. But if he can just get the social part together, he would have been able to unite the country. But his mouth is what keeps messing it up for him. If he was the president, the way he was that friend of mine, back then when he fought for me personally, I would have nothing bad to say about him.

I Find Him Racist Now

While Claudia highlights how Trump treated her in the past with respect, I wondered aloud, if she really believed he was a racist.

Claudia: I find him racist now. And I feel like, if you are pretending to be racist to get that fan base, it is almost like if you are a cop and you say I am a good cop, but you allow another cop to do something bad, and you stand by and let it happen, you are complicit in that. So, he has just said some ignorant things. Like, "That's my African-American." Can you imagine if I said, that is my Jew? First of all, Hollywood would, I would be thrown out. You know how that is here. There are just certain things you do not do; you know what I mean? I do not like it. And it sucks, because like I said there are certain things. I love the prison reform. I love the work in prison reform. I think that is amazing; we need that. He has done some good things, but his personality is messing up his presidency.

He Fired Me and Rushed to Talk About Obama's Birther

Claudia first heard about Trump birther theories right after he fired her from *The Apprentice*:

So, this is when Donald Trump had just started talking about all the birther stuff. So, I am up for elimination that day, and I feel like he rushed through the boardroom, just hurry up [and] fired me. But he said it so, it was the kindest firing ever, because he did like me. He wrapped us up quickly so he could get to his press conference, so we can talk about Barack Obama not being an American citizen. And offering this bounty if anyone can provide proof of his birth certificate, or the passport, whatever he asked for. And I was like, what are you doing? Win on your own merits if that is your plan, but to just, it is just a cheap shot. I do not think he needed to do all that. So that was the beginning of it, and just the unforced errors that he makes.

He makes errors that he does not have to make. Get off Twitter. He is emotional. So, anyone that is emotional, and they get on Twitter, they are going to say something stupid. I say something stupid, but guess what? I am not the president. So, my tweets are going to be a little more forgiven. And I just wish he would just bring it on back just a little bit. I really do. It's a shame I don't like our country being like this."

We Suddenly Love George W. Bush

Claudia came with an interesting angle:

Yeah. Remember they were pretty harsh on George Bush. And remember people thought he was the worst president ever, the dumbest president ever. And now we are at a point where now they have embraced George Bush because Donald is the newer situation. And now they love, a lot of folks love George Bush now. But yeah, I hate that everything is about Donald Trump. I think Donald Trump likes it to be like that. But we were kind of force-fed Donald Trump 24/7 and the ratings of, people got really interested in politics in the last eight to ten years, I think. Way more than before.

And I think this phenomenon of Donald Trump, he knows how to manipulate, he knows how to keep the attention on him. He is a reality star; he is a reality TV producer. He is excellent at keeping his name in your mouth, and on your mind. And I am sick of it. I am sick of dinner conversations being about Donald

Trump. I am sick of hanging out with my friends on the beach and it is Donald Trump. I am sick of it."

Trump's Central Park Five Ad

Claudia found out more about Trump's political agenda after their friendship ended:

"Not as much now. Plus, I make no secret about it, I am a liberal, I am a Democrat so most of Hollywood is as well, so it has not hurt me in that regard. But I feel it is something that people find common ground in disliking him, so it is like an icebreaker. Once you find out that they feel the same way, it is like, oh, okay. But it was really hard for me at first, because like I said I had a personal relationship with him, so I was like, damn, what I am seeing now with this person is not how he was with me. So, was it always there? Because I did not know at the time when I was friends with him. I was ignorant to the fact that he took up that full-page ad calling for the execution of the Central Park Five, which are now the exonerated five. They never raped that woman. And to call for that, when they were kids, it leaves a bad taste in my mouth.

And again, it felt like a betrayal finding out these things after the fact, after I spoke so highly of him. I have love for him, I thought that was my boy. I had been on the Trump helicopter. He picked five girls from *Deal or No Deal* to celebrate his birthday in Atlantic City, run the helicopter. I was at the US Open with him and Melania, we all sat together. We were friends. I almost wish I could see him and just shake him back to go back to how you were in the nineties. But I think he is really drunk on power right now. And it feels good [to him]. If you are a narcissist or an egomaniac, which love him or hate him, he is this, that is not a secret. He loves his ego stroked. I think what he gets from this is just the more outrageous he is, the more his base loves that. To them, he is funny, he's entertaining.

He Told My Mother: "I Made Her"

Claudia reflected about childish moments she witnessed with Trump:

I think Donald Trump wants more than anything else, for people to admire him and to love him. Because he said something the other day like, "Oh, Joe Biden will probably be the next president because a lot of people don't love me." And some people can laugh at that, but I think that was kind of a sad statement. That he feels that way. And I do not know what his relationship was with his parents. I saw a documentary recently about it, but it did not seem like it was that loving. And I have seen, I have read quotes from his mother that were not too nice. And thinking, what you lack as a child, you really want to overcompensate for when you get older. So, I think, I think that it means a lot to him to be loved, to be adored. And he likes to be praised. Even when I was friends with him, I knew, if you want Donald Trump to do you a favor, or to fight for you, just give him a compliment. Sorry Donald.

He told my mother that he made me. Yeah, he told my mother that he made me. And my mother was like, I actually made her. But he was meaning, I made you a star. Well, my career was not that big back then, I am still working on it. But it is like I said, it is too bad, because I think there are some good qualities there and some good ideas, but his personality is getting in his way.

***

Claudia wanted to add her perspective about racism:

We've been talking about this for thirty years. It has been, Rodney King, nothing has changed. Except, now we have social media, and we have cameras on our phones. So, I hate that, what happened to George Floyd, but his death will not be in vain. Because

I have never seen this many white people and allies. People getting on board and saying, I do not agree with this either. And that feels good. That gives me some kind of hope here. A lot of us are feeling like, this year started off horrible, but maybe we can end on a positive note if it brings about change, and people seeing each other as equals.

And that is one thing I think that goes back to the way I was raised, being biracial. Immigrant mother, American father that's black, and [a] military man. I was forced, I had no choice but to see the other side. And because of that I feel like it was so helpful in life to be more open-minded. I do not believe all stereotypes about every white person is this. And I try to show that every black person is not like that. There is always, we have got to start looking at the individuals. But yeah, if we keep saying, keep going where we are going, we will go nowhere. This country will continue to plummet further into the abyss and to the toilet of the world. Because right now, I am embarrassed about what we are doing right now as a country. We look terrible.

Donald, What Happened to You?

Claudia could not wrap without sending a message to her former friend:

Donald, what happened to you? Was our friendship fake? What happened to the person you were when I had love for you, and I thought you were a good person? Is this person the real you, or the other personality the real you? Stop making all these unforced errors, stop running your mouth. Pandering to 30 percent of the people is leaving 70 percent of us in the dark, in the cold. And we will not support you. You have ruined your legacy getting into politics, because when you were in television and real estate you were beloved. And if you want that love, that I think you really

need, and you desperately want, I will say get out. I would say get
out before it will be too late.

Wisdom of Trump: Dean Cain

Conservatives always appreciated the "wisdom" of the forty-fifth
president when his vocabulary would qualify for the No-No
Rhetoric from the liberal end.

Dean Cain clearly put everything into perspective with this
statement.

> President Trump will get criticized no matter what he does.
> So, if he cures cancer, they are going to be mad that he put doctors
> out of work.

Dean Cain was their second interview, and it was in Beverly Hills,
at Steven Paul's studio. Steven's wife, Jamie, was in charge with a
soundman. Plus, there was, as usual, Tim and Monica handling
cameras. All together they were seven, including Dean.

That was one of the most crowded sets. Here the studio was
big, there was extra space but during the filming there were only
necessary minimum in the room. No other interview involved
this many and that was fitting to the Covid-19 protocol.

***

Since Daphne and Erbil were both authors with newly published
books, there was more to these encounters than interviews.
After all, President Trump was everybody's favorite, and these
books were about him.

So, it was mutual interest that they would autograph their
books and take a photo with Erbil wearing one of those hats or
T-shirts engraved: "Trump GameChanger."

***

The interview with Dean Cain was interesting from various perspectives. He was Ivy League educated and came from parents in the entertainment industry.

Plus, he had self-confidence. He was not losing jobs for being a Trump loyalist or afraid of losing because of that.

He was also a professional football player. So, he had some extra qualities, making him an "All American" so to speak. In that sense, it was easy to see why he was cast as Superman.

Superman Comes Flying In

When Superman arrived at the office of Jon Voight and Steven Paul, there was some excitement in the air. Steven's wife, Jamie, asked me quietly if we could bring him up to Jon and Steven, after the filming.

I guess, we are all taken by movie heroes like "Superman."

Next, we would shoot with "Hercules" (Kevin Sorbo) and "Buffy the Vampire Slayer" (Kristy Swanson)—all action movie actors, who dared to speak about their support of Donald Trump.

In real life they are nice family people who are looking for the next good film or project.

Dean arrived in a teal green car. I was impressed!

Just when COVID-19 was taking over America, Dean Cain and Kristy Swanson made headlines for their visit at the Oval Office.

On February 27, 2020, after their show, *FBI Lovebirds*, played at CPAC, Cain and Swanson were invited to meet the president. While COVID-19 and impeachment dominated the news, some reporters sarcastically wrote about how Trump opted to spend his time that day.

But Cain (and later Swanson) would recall this afternoon differently.

The play was based on real-life anti-Trump texts between Peter Strzok and Lisa Page, the two former FBI employees, who reportedly had an affair.

Dean Cain: "Well, it's funny to me that people want to criti-cize. President Trump will get criticized no matter what he does. So, if he cures cancer, they are going to be mad that he put doc-tors out of work. No matter what he does, he always gets casti-gated by the mainstream press. So, we were there to do a play of verbatim reading of the text between Peter Strzok and Lisa Page. Of course, Peter Strzok was the number one counterintelligence agent. He was the guy working on the Russian collusion thing. These guys were so biased against the president and their texts showed that. What we found interesting in doing the play was the reaction from people. Because you have got bits and pieces of what they had said. We have heard bits and pieces of it in the media. But when you hear the way they interact with each other and the way they sound, it sounds like they are teenagers. And their hate for the president it is right there in black and white.

Is so clear. It is so obvious. And when these are the people, the lead agent and the lead lawyer going after the president and you see their bias like that. There is a reason he got kicked off the mother team. But he is one of the guys who had set up Mike Flynn. That stuff is crazy. So, when we got a chance to meet with the president. . . I have known the president for a long time. I am a great fan of his. I judged the Miss Universe. I believe it was for way back in the day. I have just known him for a long time. And I considered him a friend and I have great respect for him. And so, we got a chance to go down and sit and talk with him about the play that we were doing.

And he thought it was hysterical. He wanted to see it obvi-ously. And in his rallies, he had been doing the version of the *Lovebirds*. "Oh, Lisa, I love it." And only the way that the pres-ident can do it. And it was hysterical. It was very funny. So, we talked about that. He was extremely warm, gracious, candid. We talked about a lot of things and it was a wonderful time. I think it was February 27th or something. And the fact is, yeah, there was discussion about the coronavirus at that time, but it was not the number one situation. It was not the thing everyone was talking about. But he had already taken steps and done some things. And it was about the last CPAC.

After CPAC, a couple of weeks later, I was in New York. And then after that everything has been locked down. But the president was gracious. Sure, he met with us that, if he goes and golfs there, he should be doing this instead. If he goes tomorrow, what is he doing there? He should not be here. I mean, I do not have to tell you. He is always working. He has always got some. Even if he is golfing, he is working, the guy never stops. And I remember early in his presidency of trying to tell him he is a lazy president. He is the farthest thing from a lazy president that I have ever seen. It is crazy. But you know, in general, I think big part of the problem is that there are a huge cabal of folks who do not like him.

He has upset the apple cart, so to speak. He has come into the White House, shockingly, all these insiders, all these commies and the McCabes and Peter Strzok, and these guys who have been part of what they call the deep state. Those guys have been so entrenched in their business and their business of government that this outsider coming in, looking at it all. And this does not work, this is not right. That is not it, get out. They will do anything to take him down and we are witnessing it. However, the president, he is the Teflon Don in a sense. And I hate to use that term. But he said things most candidates could never recover from, gets away with it. It is his personality, but he has been doing this. He has been in the limelight for decades. And of course, it gives a lot of fodder to his detractors and those who do not like him, but he keeps winning.

***

Dean Cain was not an original Trump supporter.

Switching from Cruz to Trump

Well, at the time Senator Cruz had just dropped out of the race. And I was going to Senator Cruz, he's a Princeton guy like me. He is five years younger than me though. I was gone before he even got to school there. Brilliant guy, I really liked Senator Cruz quite a bit. And I felt he was going to be the strongest candidate and he dropped out. And at that point in time, President Trump, then candidate Trump, was the guy and I openly went and supported him. And boy did I get an avalanche of hate, which was hysterical, but I am so thankful that he became president. I am so thankful for what he has done for this country and internationally. And I am really looking forward to the 2020 election. If he gets four more years, I think we are in for a heck of a good ride.

So, you go and publicly endorse the candidate Donald Trump. All right, what is the response.

Well, it is so funny because the response is never about policy. So, when everybody wants to discuss policy we find we are not far apart. But there is a loathing by so many people of President Trump. They do not like his style. They do not like his tweets. They do not like that thing. So, they never ever discuss policy. They never want to discuss policy. They do not want to talk about issues. They want to talk about his demeanour, his style, his rhetoric, that is it. And that is not what it is about for me. You know, I travel the whole world as obviously, as you do. And I see and talk to people of all different faith's cultures, races, governments, and I see how they react in some places. You will see, they have pictures of their leaders and things and so on and so forth.

And in the United States, I will walk around with a picture of the Constitution because that is what really holds court in the United States. We all live under the Constitution. The president is a figurehead. And I did not support Barack Obama for president, but once he was president, he is my president. I want him to do well because I want the United States to do well. And people cannot now. It is the strangest thing to see. President Trump is doing and working so hard for this country. But people from Bill Maher to, I could run the list. Bill Maher rooting for a recession to get rid of Trump. You are rooting to hurt the livelihoods of millions of people to get Trump out of the White House because you do not like him. I mean, that is insane. It is a definition of insanity.

It does not make any sense to me at all. There is no compassion. They're so hypocritical. It is unreal. Because they just do not like the man. I do not know what it is about President Trump that they do not like so much. And maybe they do not like that he is brash, that he is a little rough when he does not lie. He is a counterpuncher from New York. I mean, you take a shot at construction. I mean, I know some, I know some big-time construction folks and they can all get in the muck and mire and they get it done. And the president is a counterpuncher and they just do not like him.

Yeah, that certainly could be part of it because Hollywood likes to be loved and needed and likes to think that their influence extends through politics and everything else in pop culture. A lot of it does, however, it is proven that people . . . I think it goes back to Bill Clinton, it is the economy, stupid. That is, it. It is the economy. It really is the economy. When people have money and things and employment and they are gainfully employed and things are going, I think then you can think about things that are less important, then you start to nitpick things like that.

The president does not need Hollywood. They have turned it into this and us versus them thing. That is polarized Hollywood, but it has not translated to votes. It did not translate to votes for Hillary Clinton at all. She won with over three million of the popular votes. Well, because California has a huge number of people.

Popular Vote

We do not win by the popular vote. It is like in football. I do not care how many yards rushing you have. I care what the score is at the end. That is the electoral college. There is a reason for the electoral college. If you look at the counties that President Trump won in 2016 and you just color them in, if you looked at a color map, and I am sure you can find one of these anywhere, it is a very red country. If you put red and blue. Only certain areas were blue, but there was a high concentration of people.

I do not know what it is. Maybe they do not like . . . There are certain countries . . . In England, when someone achieves success in England, they love to tear them down. I was talking to some of my English friends. One of the things they love about America is we celebrate success. I want to be like that. I want to be able to achieve that.

Beyonce, Jay-Z, De Niro

Mentioning the names of A-listers who opposed Donald Trump loudly sits okay with Dean Cain. If he had been hurt by some of Hollywood elite, he managed to sound gracious.

Dean: Beyoncé and Jay-Z, I don't agree with their politics very much, but bless them. They are hugely successful. I want to have that kind of success. I would aspire to do that. I would not want to tear them down. Jay-Z is now doing things with the NFL. Again, it would not be my choice, but good for him. I celebrate their success. People celebrated Donald Trump's success for a long time until he became president, and then now they've gone after him.

***

Dean and I weighed other angles of Trump vs. Hollywood: Would the fact that Donald Trump mastered the news around the clock, since he had announced he was running for president, take attention off other big names?

He jumped on it:

Dean: The President has, he has certainly sucked the air out of the room in that sense. Incredibly entertaining. For a guy who sits and does the news, I do *Fox & Friends* and I host the shows and interview folks, and to watch the pace at which things move with President Trump at the helm is unreal. I have never seen anything like it. When I talk to my colleagues, they say the same thing. It is warp speed. Is this the new normal? I do not know. I cannot see that being the case. It is just unique to President Trump. He is an enigma, without a doubt.

I would say, this is something that I, without a doubt, I have never seen someone take so much incoming fire from people who do not like him and be so resolute and steadfast in doing what I believe is the right thing. He does it all the time. Whenever I get a chance to see him [and] speak with him, I always just thank him for what he has done in the face of all this incredible opposition. I am an ideal guy and policy guy. The things that he puts in place, I agree with. Small government. I am a small government person. I am for individual liberties. I am for things that this country was founded upon. These are the things he stands up for it. That is why it resonates so much with so many Americans.

Look, we all like . . . I like watching movies with X, Y, or Z person. I think De Niro is a fine actor. I enjoy watching his movies. I do not care for his politics much, but I can still enjoy his films. Jim Carrey. I think he is a fantastic actor. I like him as a person. I would not put any of my trust . . . I would not want him to babysit my kids or anything. Not that he would be . . . I do not agree with any of his politics and I think he does some ugly things politically, but I still like his movies. You know what I mean? I can separate the two. A lot of people cannot separate those things. Their hate for the president is so strong that when he does something that is wonderful, they cannot even give him credit.

We do not hear about other stories, involving Donald Trump. . .It is surprising. The stories of the kindness . . . You hear so many stories of the kindness of President Trump just as a human being all the time. Obviously, he cannot do that stuff as much now because he is the president. It makes sense. He is the leader of the free world. You hear those stories of him . . . I am not surprised by any of them. He has always been such a warm, caring person, 100 percent, but you do not see that often portrayed in the media. All you see is him fending off Jim Acosta [of CNN] or some silly things like that.

Threats

I'm a grown man. Threaten me and I will react in kind. We will see. The kind of threats that I got . . . What are they going to send me? "I am not going to put you in my movies." That is discrimination. It is illegal. Plus, nobody in Hollywood has the balls to say that to someone's face. I am afraid that is just the straight way it is.

I am sure it has happened. I cannot prove it, do not care for it. I do not care. I literally do not care. I think there is a big pendulum swing, and the pendulum swings around. I think there is a big pendulum swing coming back.

You even look at the things like when Brett Kavanaugh was being confirmed and all the things that went on and you hear them just lauding Dr. Blasey-Ford about how she was so credible and all these things. There were a lot of things we found out in her testimony . . . Her testimony was very weak and very odd and strange. I happen to have some insight because I happen to know her ex-boyfriend very well. I grew up with him. His letter blew apart so much of her story. He has no dog in that race. He does not care. In fact, he did not want to have anything to do with it.

There was a whole lot of baloney in that and the things that she was claiming. It was shocking.

Suddenly, you see now it is "believe all women," blah, blah, blah, blah, this sort of thing. Suddenly, someone has an allegation against Joe Biden, and it is, "it may be true, but I am still going to support Joe Biden to get rid of Trump." It just shows the hypocrisy. That is Hollywood. That is the media. There are so many folks who do that. It is stunning to me, but that hypocrisy is being exposed more and more and more and more. I just feel like it is only a matter of time before the bright lights shine upon so many others. You look at the support they gave to Harvey Weinstein and that situation. I mean, it is stunning to me.

Listen, Hollywood is not a moral town. You know this. I am stating the obvious. It is a bottom line, dollar, the bottom dollar . . . It is all about the bottom line. How much money is there in that? How much power is there in doing this? That is what Hollywood is about. If Dwayne Johnson came out and said, "I'm a staunch Trump supporter," he is the highest paid actor in films now, he can do whatever he wants. He is untouchable in that sense. Jon Voight is so talented and done so well. You cannot stop Jon from working. Me, I've been able to work tons and tons.

Blacklisting

It is a terrifying concept, but it is so brazenly accepted within Hollywood that they cannot even see their own hypocrisy. When that [Debra Messing] tweet went out, and then Eric McCormack said something supporting it like "Yes, we want to know. So, we know who not to work with," I answered that tweet openly and I said, "I am going to be out of town filming, but I will let you know right now if I were in town, I would love to have been attending that. So, you can put my name front and center." Facing that and calling it what it was, was what I was trying to do.

I am not scared that Debra Messing and Eric McCormack think that my support for the president is a reason not to work. . .

Do not work with me then. By the way, say that to my face, explain to me why that is not okay. Blacklisting and that stuff is disgusting. It is an illegal thing to do, to not hire someone because of their political persuasions. You want to talk about civil rights and the first amendment? These people, they do not see the hypocrisy of what they are saying. So, is there an attempt to blacklist Hollywood actors who support the president? Probably. It is underhanded, they do not have the guts to put it out front and center.

I have never heard it to my face, but people have quietly talked to me about things. I sit in the board of directors for the NRA. I am a reserve police officer. I am openly out there with my ideas and ideals and why, but I will discuss them with anyone, and I am happy to. There is a reason I am a reserve police officer; I did that because I support law enforcement. Now is every law enforcement officer perfect? No. Are mistakes made? Yes. Have I had negative contact with law enforcement? Yes, I have, and it makes you very angry and there's ways to deal with that. But I wear my heart on my sleeve in a sense. They love to pick on me for being an actor. I think that is funny. "We want to hear what an actor has to say," but then they dig a little further and they're like, "He's some stupid act. . . Oh, he went to Princeton? Oh, okay. All right, so he's not that stupid, but he's probably still pretty stupid." Or "What does he know about this? Oh, he played in the NFL. Oh, okay. Well, he maybe knows a little bit about this."

And then they started looking at, "What does he know about international politics? Oh, he's travelled to make documentaries." Then they start looking at things like, "Oh, maybe he does know." They do not even pay attention. They just call you the stupid actor without paying attention. As I have gotten older, I have gotten more interested in the world because I am a father and my son's going to be in this world. And I understand, and I have seen how bad policy has affected countries because I have been to them and seen it.

I have shot five, six movies in Bulgaria, starting in 1997. And it was a different country back then. And to see how it has evolved is wonderful, but it is shocking. So, I must be involved in politics and voice my opinion, because. . . What was that saying? "You may not be interested in politics, but I promise you politics are interested in you and it's going to affect you." So, I am having to impart this to my son and to his friends and the other college kids out there. And I speak in colleges, I am happy to go speak to the kids and talk to them, but I will talk to them about listening to the other side, having a respectful dialogue, and hopefully we will see more of that taking place. But I really do believe the pendulum is going to swing back. And a lot of these rats that have been in the cupboard are going to be exposed. And I think it is going to be a good thing for the country.

Not a Racist

I have seen nothing that would even suggest that Donald Trump is a racist. It is insane to me. Even back in the days where he was being lauded by the NAACP and getting awards for this and that and the other. I have been called a racist all the time.

I think that is unfortunate. I think it is bigoted. And I think people, they throw that word around, bigot. I do not think they really know what it means. So, if you just cannot be friends with somebody because their political opinion is different than yours, you are a bigot. Sorry? It is a bad word because it is a bad thing to do and it is a bad way to be. Like the fact that this person said that their daughters would never talk to them is shocking, it is shocking to me. I will be in the makeup trailer doing something, and this has been for years, you hear people talking, "Oh, this blah, blah, blah." I will go, "Well, actually I support President Trump. Let us talk about it and we'll get it out there." And it is the shock on people's faces that they are like, "You openly are just saying you support [Trump]."

"100 percent, absolutely. Let us discuss it." "Well, how could he say this?" Talk policy. Do not worry about what he says . . . I am not so worried about that stuff. I want to know what his policies are. How does he lead? I do not expect him to be a saint. I know world leaders. I know people. They are not saints. None of them. And to be an effective leader you must have your priorities in check, and you got to know how to lead. And president is leading, and he is leading very well.

The idea that people are afraid to talk about that is, it is just shocking to me. And that is cowardly to be honest. But I understand how people do not want to. . . . Listen, it does color people's perceptions of you, it does. Again, I think that is the pendulum thing. I think it's going to come back around where people will look back at this and go "Wow. For someone like me, Dean said what he thought. And he stuck with his convictions. Turns out in the long run, he still sticks with those convictions and they were the right thing for the country." And I think that is what I think will happen for those who are out speaking their mind. Jon Voight, Kristy, myself. I think that we will be proven right. I certainly hope that's the case because I think they're the right ideals.

Hate on Twitter

And how could we discuss Trump without mentioning the social media platform which perhaps made him a president, and would later ban him?

Dean: I get so much hate on Twitter that I actually see it as a badge of honor in some ways. I'll even say to my son beforehand, "Hey, this is my tweet right here. Watch what happens." And I will tweet it out and you see when the organized groups come after you. And it is hysterical. It has happened to me six, ten times, and that is okay. I am a big boy. I can handle it. Listen, I am not able to give the president any advice on how to handle things. I would just tell him to do what he is already doing. Stay the course. Stay the course and hold onto the policies that you put in place to do the right things for this country.

And in the end, I think history will be very kind to President Trump and the decisions he has made. He was talking today about even Syria, "Oh my gosh, we've done all these horrible things. We've pulled out." You do not hear anything anymore. We have twenty-seven soldiers there, for the love of God, and the things that are going on there are still going on there. And we do not hear about it anymore. It is the amazing things that happened, he gets castigated and then it is gone. And then it is on to the next thing. It is on to the next thing. It is onto the next thing. And they forget. Except that now video lives forever. So, these people who were hammering him for X, Y, or Z were hammering Kavanaugh for that situation. Here we are not two years later, and they are all changing their tunes. It is amazing. So, my advice to the president would be stay the course and do what is right for America. DO what he knows and believes is right. And in the end, history will be very kind.

What the Doctor Ordered: Isaiah Washington

Then, there was Isaiah Washington. He stood out as well among two dozen interviewees but for more reasons than one can think of.

First, he was the only "doctor" interviewed by Daphne. "Doctor Preston Burke," that is!

Isaiah was very vocal about Trump, about Hollywood, but also on discrimination and racism.

> What I have seen with the media, who is notorious for having nasty, dirty, lowlife, "Hollyweird" behavior attack this man because he is

the president, I began to put it together. He knows their secrets and all those hotel nights. I would be a little nervous, too.

—Isaiah Washington

Doctor Preston Burke

"I see you included Isaiah," a media owner said to me after watching the trailer for *Trump vs. Hollywood*. "How did you two get along with him?"

The actor who is still known to many for playing Doctor Preston Burke in the medical drama, *Grey's Anatomy*, has been described as "difficult" by some in the industry, after being fired from the series, due to reportedly using a homophobic slur on the set.

Much has been written about it, and Isaiah himself seems hurt whenever one mentions it to him after thirteen years.

Yes, he did have some unexplainable angry moments and texts. Yet, he appeared on the set, on time, after asking about the dress code. His voice was going from whispering louder, louder. . . then whispering again. His body language was engaging. The man knows how to give a good show.

He also knows how to give a compliment: He tweeted that "Daphne Barak and her team did an excellent job" after the film was out for pre-screening. He texted me similar compliments and asked me to consider supporting a couple of his other films.

But then, with him, there is always the "extra drama."

While filming, Bill and the crew were uneasy when Isaiah decided to talk about sexual misconduct in Hollywood, mentioning A-listers we knew. I tried to keep a normal expression, while directing the conversation back to Trump vs. Hollywood.

Yet, Isaiah was talking about what was obviously bothering him. Being the smart man he is, Isaiah knew we could never air such content. Maybe it was his way to share his unpleasant moments in Hollywood anyway?

After leaving these parts on the (editing) floor, I am happy we included him. Interesting man, passionate actor, proud American, proud African American. He resents being "boxed in."

Isaiah: I grew up, I became a man in Houston, a young man in Houston. I became a military younger man [in the Air Force] that could follow orders from ages eighteen to twenty-one. I grew up as a man in New York. I have been knocked out, accused of being gay, and abused, doing wilding out, period. I was angry like private citizen Donald Trump as well. I was wanting law and order as well. I wanted the corruption of the police office to go away as well. [Director] Ava DuVernay does not follow me on Twitter anymore. She blocked me because I do not believe in that story of Central Five. I was there. I had been abused by people that looked like me. When it first started out, it was kind of cool, like a bunch of kids are fighting racism and corrupt cops and they are going after people because they are on this Nat Turner thing. When it started out. But like any movement or any intent, it gets co-opted and corrupted. It was not until I got attacked by people that looked like me and mugged me that I woke up on the number 2 train coming from the Bronx, or the number 3, wherever it was, trying to get back to Brooklyn that I realized this has nothing to do with politics. This is just thuggery.

I supported Trump when he came up with that. I wanted vengeance as well. Yeah. Put them down. I do not care who did it. Put them down. Because I am suffering from bad cops. I am suffering from bad Italian guys. I am suffering. I am tired of the thugs, period. My point of view and perspective from living there at that time, I was on the same page as billionaire Donald Trump. I also remember everybody was rapping around about Donald Trump. Everybody wanted to be Donald Trump. He came in and saved the skating rink when no one else can figure it out. He is about beauty. He is clear on it. He does not even like to keep the same wife when he does not think she is attractive anymore. I mean, he has just been very clear about that. He's like, "I messed up. We may have children." He is never hiding that. We all knew that about him. We all knew that.

Not Racist

I never saw him as a bigot or a racist because I never saw that when he got behind Jesse Jackson, twice. I was in New York when all these things were happening. No, I am not going to sit here and say, "Oh, I think he's a racist," because I have not seen him . . . The definition of a racist is I am not trying to help you at all because of who you are. I have never seen that. That is a lot.

To go to your point, it was not until I was at the White House, to see the man that I sort of grew up with in New York, from the ages of twenty-five to thirty-three, all the years I lived in New York and watching him and just being a New Yorker, I saw the man that I respected, that I was familiar with back in New York. It was at that point where I realized, oh my God, he is being treated and being cancelled just like they try to do to me.

It was at that point, after I saw my tweet being taken out of context, when I decided, okay, you want to play? You want to see a black conservative? Man. I am about to give you the most incredible black conservative in the history of black conservatives. Because you do not know me. You do not know that I grew up in a conservative Frederick Douglass loving, Ida B. Wells loving, John F. Keane, Martin Luther King, Robert F. Kennedy loving community with white coaches on the football team. You do not understand. I am a different kind of man. I am going to show you. You made a mistake. You made a mistake.

When I get behind my president of the United States, watch how many people start listening in a different kind of way. I have only done it in a year. You have not seen nothing yet. I am just getting started. Blacklisting, like when Donald Trump was campaigning here, they were fundraising, so Debra Messing and all kind of Hollywood characters say, "Let's see who is going here and let's blacklist them." Right? I am thinking, Debra Messing? I went after her on Twitter with that. I went after the other guy too. They did not tweet at me. They fear me because I got too many MAGA followers now.

You have to understand . . . People say this and I have said this and out of context, it is like, oh, he is the most arrogant person. I do not give a crap about what you think about me. I am confident because I have earned it. I have served this country and I served it well. I was not during a war time, but I raised my hand. I love this country. It has been exceptionally good to me. I mean that.

Yes, do we have issues? Do we have problems? Yes, we have conflict. But you know what? If you took all of the black people and took all the women off the planet, these white men will still find a way to kill each other. It has been proven. Go look at *Braveheart*. They do not need us. . . . You do not need me to kill. Look at the *Purge* movies. That is just a DNA thing.

I believe that DNA of people that believe in civility and peace will find a way to work it out. That is where civilization comes into play. History tells me that there was a time where you had the Dark Ages and the black plague, and then you have other people that want to come in and go, "You know what, guys? Maybe we should not be sleeping with animals and throwing feces and urine on top of each other's hands. Maybe we should clean up a little bit. Right?" Kind of like now. Wash your hands! Okay? If you do not, things like bubonic plague shows up. Okay? It is your behavior.

What I have seen with the media, who is notorious for having nasty, dirty, lowlife, "Hollyweird" behavior attack this man because he is the president, I began to put it together. He knows their secrets and all those hotel nights. I would be a little nervous, too. Of course, I am not going to be excited about anybody that knows all my dirt. Would you? Become the most powerful person in the world.

Absolutely, Jeffrey Zucker, you make that guy a monster, make him a monster yesterday. But guess what? They underestimated the electoral college. Fifty-three get delegates out of California, all the delegation in New York, not enough gerrymandering, and fraud because the people decided for the last fifty years or however, we have not seen you guys really do anything for us in the last twenty years on either side of the fence. Let us just throw another guy in there that we know knows how to build some shit.

Also, bankruptcy is not a bad word. You are entitled to it. If you are a businessperson. . . .You have a right. Every year, every company. It is a right. Let us get that straight.

. . . if you say monster and the monster become the president, than you cannot stop saying he is a monster because you have created another monster. I am still a homophobic villain. No matter all the good things. . . . DUI, domestic violence, nothing. I have written books. I am a media blackout. It is like, I cannot make you the good guy because . . . must be the good guy and he has a British accent, and he looks like you! That is a novel idea. He is a nicer Isaiah.

Hollywood

Hollywood is the media. They are interconnected. You do not go anywhere, unless you are working as a renegade or an outsider . . . The renegades used to the outsiders. [Steven] Spielberg, [Martin] Scorsese, [Brian] De Palma, and there is another guy with the glasses, I forget his name. They were outsiders, too, when we had movies like *Easy Rider*. The good old days when we had the progressive movies where, wow, they are telling some really great stories and Jack Nicholson. Cary Grant, because he was open with his sexuality, they hated him for seasoning with men and women, hated him for it. Hated that he wanted to be with the guy that is like . . . What is his . . . Not Gary Cooper, but he was a famous Western TV star.

Cary Grant certainly was. This guy. I read his book. The reason why they hated him and never give them an Oscar is because they could not control him. He wore stockings. He was always immaculate. He was always elegant and was always clean. I love Cary Grant. I used to consider myself a dark Cary Grant when I was on *Grey's*. They just did not want to let it happen. They had news. They're like, "No, no. George Clooney is going to be that. Not you." I mean, I can do . . . The president [of the network] told me. I said, "Once I leave *Grey's*, can I be like Cary Grant?"

Steve McPherson [president of ABC Entertainment] said, "Oh, no." He told him at the upfronts, a reporter, he says, "He ain't going nowhere." This was during the upfronts. The reporter said, "What do you mean by that?" He says, "Look at Isaiah's ankle. Look down on his ankle." We looked at my ankle. Nothing there. He says, "Don't you see the fucking shackle down there?"

We're looked upon as property. If you are a black person, you are less than property. Look how they treat their women. As soon as you age out, you got to play a mother, or you do not get your eight million. Unless you are Meryl Streep. They decide who gets the bag based on whatever they have done. You are not going to go forward. The media and Hollywood work hand in hand is what we are saying.

It was not my fault. I did not know I was as powerful as I was. Louis Gossett played a doctor called Lazarus something and then he kissed a white woman in the seventies on a TV show on CBS. They had . . . so they wrote him off the show.

Probably the biggest sets that I have ever been on, in 2005 was a lot of the people that came out of Santa Clarita at that time that did not know that there were doctors that were black, let alone a surgeon. I had to bring a real African American heart surgeon to the set, to my own crew. Matter of fact, Mark Pedowitz, who is now the CEO of CW network, had to fire three cameramen because they refused to light me. Not only could they refuse to light me, but they also did not know how to light a dark-skinned man in blue scrubs. Mark Pedowitz said, "Look, I have three black people in my show. I want to be able to see them." We shot six-day weeks, eighteen days, three crews, until we found someone that I finally told him, "You know what, you need to put a certain gauge of film of that height." I forget the number.

Apology . . .

Isaiah *did* apologize about improper language. He said: "I will apologize for my comments to the Golden Globe. You do not drink for four hours at the Golden Globe and do not go use a word, whether you are telling the truth, whatever the context, and use a word that you are being crucified for in the news for three months. No. I was cashed out.

I was cashed out because everybody in control realized they could not have sex with me. I was a heterosexual. This is the truth. I broke the fantasy.

They made up a story where the entire head got fired. What they did not understand is when you fired the head of wardrobe, the whole crew. . . So, we were left with one person to dress all of us. And I watched them as little kids wield this power, wield this axe. I said, chopped off all these heads coming to me now. I am going to go to be the sage now and fix it. And I said, "No. This is what power does. And this is what abuse of power yields. Live with it.

"I Know Lady Melania's Pain . . ."

I am operating in support of Trump out of love for humanity. I do not like how they are treating the president of the United States. Who also, I might add in case you forget about it, is a father like me? Is a husband like me? God knows, cares what he does in his private life. But Lady Melania, the first lady and his wife, I know the pain of what my wife goes through to this day. When people accusing me of being something I am not. It does not hurt her because our lives are great. But for our kids, we must educate them on why this is happening. So, they are strong, they are inoculated. I know how a lie works. We are still talking about race. Not because I brought it up because however you bring it up, it is a part of the conversation.

But the good thing is, is the residuals are great. Cause everyone is sitting up and discovering the show. "Oh my God, oh my God!" I got shows out there that the residuals go down. This is the one job where the residuals, it is a gift that keeps on giving, thank God. Sometimes rejection is God's protection in my book.

Now you are dealing with a medium and you are dealing with an industry that has attracted traumatized godless people who have been hurt. They have been rejected out of their Southern homes as children, they are in their sixties and seventies now, kicked in their behinds by their Marine fathers, back in Mississippi, Georgia, and Louisiana, Texas. Had to flee to New York during the Andy Warhol days, find their community, find their voice and then come out here and say, "You know what? Now that we are in power and control, we can have a say."

I do not fault that. I think that is great. Freedom. I am about freedom. But when that freedom becomes corrupt and you are hurting other people, I am sure when Hitler started, he thought he was about freedom too. As a socialist, as a socialist, he was a socialist, right? I am sure Stalin felt the same way. I am about freedom for what I believe in. But then suddenly it turns a corner.

Now people are locked in their homes. People are just being left to die in New York. Black people.

It starts looking like a culling. It starts looking like another form of ethnic cleansing. This jacket is black. I am not black, Jack. I am me. I am me. Why? Because I have earned it. I am a human being first. If you do not care to see me as a human being, that is your problem, not mine. If you want to see all these other labels, that is cool. We can play that game. If you want to be white, I will be black. But at the end of the day, whether to break it down to be Israeli or Mbundu, we were people.

Fox News: New Trump Supporter

On April 2, 2019, it suddenly became public that Isaiah supported Trump. Did it scare him? Would his career in Hollywood be affected?

Isaiah: Are you kidding me? You serious? Oh, the answer to that? I have been impacted. I have been working outside of Hollywood for the last thirteen years. I have made over $5 million on my own without Hollywood and a single studio. I produce my own content. People do not know that unless you Google my name on Netflix or iTunes, I own my content. I am confident because they forced me to become the very conservative that I always was. This time leave me be the man that my grandmother will be proud of and I am.

But was he scared?

Isaiah: "One, if I am scared, ever, someone is going to die. I am not good at being afraid. I have no use for it. If I am afraid of you or anything, someone is going to be really, really, someone is not going to walk away. That is how I am trained by my grandmother, I just told you. She was not afraid of anyone or anything. So, I do not give too much.

I think Roosevelt said the most, the worst, the biggest thing that you can fear is fear itself. I think he said something like that, or I am really making it up. I look at that as that, I am the kind of person that if I am afraid, that is a horrible, horrible, horrible sensation. I do not know what that is because I do not want to be in that space. I take that very seriously. So, when I see the fear mongering and I see what the media is doing, and I see what Hollywood is doing, making people afraid by being abusers of their power. No, I was never scared. I was disappointed. I was shocked. I was dismayed. I was hurt. I was embarrassed. This lies.

I was like, what am I going to do? But then as Mark Pedowitz and I leave, he got removed, fired, but he got money. I did not. By Disney. And we licked each other's wounds for three months and I disappeared. I'm like, "I don't want to talk about this anymore. I don't want to be hurt anymore." I do not understand. He does not understand that. He is a good guy. He still is, we are still friends. I love Mark Pedowitz. And he did the best he could to try to put the same millions back in my pocket by five years, until I realized the environment got toxic and . . . and I had to leave. When there's toxicity and fear, I know enough now that if this room was on fire, I am not going to be sitting here trying to fight the fire for you. I am going to find an exit. I already know where the exits are. I know. Okay? So, I do not like fear.

"I Would Tell Trump: Now You Know How I Feel . . ."

Now you know how I feel. Because I remember watching the telly and he did not know what was going on. And the reason why I had to take more time because I had to heal. I watched him tell the reporter, but not really knowing the facts when they asked him, do you think Isaiah should be fired for what he said? And his response was, "Absolutely. Immediately. He should be fired." I was like, "Dude, you're Donald Trump. The whole world respects what you say. You just killed me, in addition to everyone else. And I love and respect you."

So, if I got to sit next to Donald Trump, I could happily say, "Now you know how I feel. I don't hold it against you because you had misinformation." And now that I see what they are doing with him, not saying he is a perfect human being, but I see something that is unfair.

So, I do not care about the past. I see injustice and I do not care if you are the president of the United States or are a home-less person that I must drive by, that I am going to pull over to find out why you do not have more. . . . It is unjust. And I am going to fight for your freedom.

Idiosyncrasies of Hollywood

Over time, the idiosyncrasies of Hollywood became too much for everyone in America. Yet disliking President Trump, lack of a better word, did not let its ills suddenly disappear. Not represent-ing values dear to all Americans and as a result constantly losing market share in the world were glaringly apparent to everyone who loved movies.

Add to that what the #MeToo movement brought to the table! It was about time real equality between men and women was established before delving into an even bigger problem involving racial tensions and problems.

Everyone would agree that "make-believe problem" of Trump persona would surely rank third after these eternal and existen-tial issues.

Let us not forget for a minute, while the Trump Persona might have been a good excuse for lots of people, race was the reason for the Civil War that killed nearly a million Americans.

***

Hollywood had been liberal in America for the past half cen-tury. At the beginning, it was patriotic and preaching common values until about 1960s, or so it seemed. Ever since, it started to lean towards left and finally in 2016 came out in full force against what it stood for when it first started its path towards world dominance.

Nowadays, Hollywood faces a tough challenge from a dozen major movie markets around the world. The decay continues unabated irrespective of the toxic political divide and COVID-19.

***

During the filming, it became most apparent that Hollywood had no tolerance whatsoever and it was in a very confused state. Never mind ignoring half of America that was adhering to a conservative political viewpoint, Hollywood was preaching "my way or the highway" and was no longer representative.

At this stage, unless Hollywood comes to terms and embraces the #MeToo movement, and then establishes a long-term strategy, history will be rewritten by those other than themselves, including three of the fastest-rising powers in the East: China, India, and Turkey. The joke of Scott Baio on the Civil War will be on America and until then idiosyncrasies of the likes of Brett Ratner will occupy everyone for no good reason.

Civil War: Scott Biao

When Scott Baio made his comment in April 2020, there was no Civil War in sight to speak of. The Civil War became part of the documentary on November 4, the day after the presidential elections when the results did not confirm who won the race.

"If there is a Civil War, do not forget who has all the guns."

In other words, presidential elections for the second time in a row did not allow a clear path out of the woods for America from the entangled mess it got itself since the breakup of the Soviet Union in the early 1990s. Hence, *Struggling for One America*, over time, has become the single most important task for every-one to focus on.

Scott Baio (Chilly) Predictions

Starting to film during COVID-19 was done with much back-and-forth internal debates. A voluminous production that would give much needed jobs in shut-down Hollywood. It would dis-cuss the growing division in America, engaging popular voices, which would trigger a wider conversation. The budget and cast-ing were there.

On the other hand, a production during such a fast-spread-ing pandemic, where many details about it are still question marks for the science world, dictated that we could not make any errors.

That meant that we used our usual film crews, who we knew were abiding by the isolation and safety rules, even between shoots. We also flew them around, instead of choosing a much cheaper solution, and hiring local freelance.

At the first couple of shoots, I even asked Doctor David Tang to accompany us and ensure the scene was safe before, during, and after the filming.

As much as we were all excited to work on this project, some shared their fears, which we encouraged.

Actor Robert Davi, who has a baby at home, chose to film in his garden, avoided the mike, which resulted in a great interview content wise. But we needed to pay a lot for sound correction, in order not to leave the footage out.

The first one to jump was actor Scott Baio. He is known as Chachi Arcola from the sitcom *Happy Days* and its spin-off *Joanie Loves Chachi*.

Steven Paul called Scott with me and invited him on behalf of Jon Voight and all of us to come and film in their offices.

In a locked down California, location became a major topic.

Scott was happy to do it but was not thrilled to drive far from his home. He suggested his friend who owned a studio, Damascus Road Productions, nearby.

Ryan from the production studio was nervous about finding camera crews during the pandemics, though grateful for the job.

We calmed him down, assuring him that we have our inhouse crews.

He came to meet with us, confessing he did not know what soft drink he had in the refrigerator because "We were closed for weeks."

We accommodated each other, chatting about our tough times, when Scott joined us with his pretty daughter, Bailey Deluca Baio.

Looking back at this casual afternoon, I cannot believe some of the things Scott said. Back in spring 2020, the smiling actor had sort of predicted the scary—almost Civil War optics—attack of January 6, 2021 on the Capitol. He talked about the danger of "censorship social media," as if he had a premonition about the banning of Donald Trump's accounts following the January 6 bloody scene at the Capitol building.

Nothing Like the First Interview

It was odd to go to the address Scott gave us. First, we also had an anxiety about going anyplace we were not familiar with, because of the COVID-19 pandemic. It should have been a lesson for us there on. In retrospect, it was not. We felt the anxiety and made sure the next time that we will not go to a place that we did not know. Instead, we will bring everybody to where we were comfortable.

Go figure! We never thought how they will feel. We simply thought they will be happy to follow us. Nonetheless, we did it our way from there on. All other interviews took place where we decided with two exceptions. Two of the twenty-four did not allow us the make the rules or to pick the spots.

Considering we filmed some of the interviews at the home of the stars and producers, it is natural they would make the rules. Two of them did while the other two did not. They let us decide in their home how we should fix it for filming. We did well with all four at-home interviews. But the two that we did not have much say in were not as comfortable as we were during Scott's interview.

We were always very conscious how many people were in the room at any one time. That everybody had their masks, and everybody was staying six feet from one another. Other than that, the room had to be ventilated. The rest was piece of cake, one would say.

We ran all our operations like a dictatorship, so we did not have any problem. The rule was there was one rule. One of us was deciding every single thing on location.

They were all decent people. In Scott's case, his daughter was there, too, but she was outside. Inside the room there were two camera people operating four cameras and sound. Then we had our doctor and his son present as an assistant. Yet they were not in the immediate area, looking on from a distance.

But First: Civil War

In the course of a relaxed long interview, Scott was chatty about some gossipy interactions with Donald and Melania Trump at the White House, sharing colorful anecdotes including jokes.

I would be asked about one of them by the reporters from the *Hollywood Reporter*, *Yahoo*, the *Daily Express* and others who gave great coverage for the filming, because we included Scott's joke in the film trailer.

Note: Scott's interview took place in the spring—weeks before the death of George Floyd and the outrage it sparked around the country. Back then, who would even entertain a thought of such a disturbing attempt to stop the electoral counting in the Senate, by violence?

Donald Trump felt secure he would be reelected. The pandemic took over the country, but few among Trump' supporters believed it would be that devastating and long-lasting.

So, when Scott made his joke, it—violence all over America and its capital—seemed so surreal, that it was a great dark joke.

He said: "First of all, if you're not hiring me because I'm a conservative, shame on you, imagine if it were reversed. And if there is a Civil War, don't forget who has all the guns."

The trailer was posted and got almost eighty thousand clicks on October 13.

Scott Baio: Between then and now? Between Reagan and Trump? There is a lot more hate right now. I think people are . . . there is a lot more violence about all this right now, and the violence is not coming from us, it is coming from the other side. I always knew that the media was slanted left, even way back when I was a boy, and I really was not even paying attention.

But the media is gone. Media is just a cheerleading squad for the Democratic Party, and I have never seen such an obvious display of partisanship in my life. No matter was the president, no matter what President Trump does . . . We have a joke, Trump could cure cancer and they would get mad at Trump for putting doctors out of business.

But I think the big difference is the parties. Back then Democrats and Republicans, they fought on taxes, and they fought on a couple of things. Now, they are so left. I mean, it's not even left, it borders on communism, and I think that's the big change.

You know what, Daphne? For Reagan, I remember people going, "Oh heck, he won. Oh well." It was not a big deal. And now, it is just a huge deal.

It bothers me that people will not speak to me because I am a Trump guy.

***

I asked Scott, bluntly, if he lost specific roles, since he announced he was supporting Trump.

Scott: Maybe I'll even do it with you, I had a network executive write something to me about all this, and it was such a horrible thing to say about not wanting to hire me. And I am going to get that out, I am going to drop the name and everything, not now, but in an email. And I thought, "How bold."

I do not really get Hollywood, but the Hollywood people are much . . . Well, you can see it on Twitter, I mean, they are just brutal and hateful. Because personally I do not hate anybody unless you give me a reason to hate, and I will talk to anybody; they will not talk to us.

But that's fascism, by the way. They want to shut us down, and they do not want any dissension, any dissent.

Twitter/Facebook Censorship in America

And then came a remark which would become so different months later, after Twitter, Facebook, Instagram, YouTube, and other social media platforms banned Donald Trump and some of his supporters who reportedly called for violence.

Scott: I want my daughter to live in the country that I grew up in. I want her to have opportunities, I want her to be free.

And I think a lot of that is going away. You see it with Facebook censoring, Twitter censors only conservatives, and I want her to be in a country that is secure and safe and prosperous. And, in my opinion, the other side does not want that. They want people dependent on government, and I do not want that life for her.

The first part of your question, I did not care how [the "joke"] backfired, and it did, I guess I will never know to what extent. And I said in an interview, I said, "If I never work again and he wins, I'm fine. I don't care."

***

Scott was relaxing, and reminiscing about how we was picked to speak at the RNC convention in 2016. Funny story.

Scott: I was at a fundraiser at a house in Beverly Hills [real estate investor Tom Barrack], and maybe there was, I don't know, fifty people, seventy-five people. [Trump] was not [yet] president, he was at a podium, and I was ten, twelve feet away from him, and he was going on, and talking to people, and this and that. And as he was coming off, I went to shake his hand and I said, "Mister Trump." And he said, "Scott Baio."

He says, "How you are doing?" Because I had met him prior to that at the Trump Plaza on Fifth Avenue. And he says, "Scott Baio, did you want to talk?"

And I went, "What?" And I thought he meant here. And he said, "Did you want to talk? Speak at the convention?" I went . . . And he grabbed me in a headlock, did not hurt me, like a guy, and he walked me . . . I was with my wife, and he walked me, grabbed me nice, walked me in . . . he was going inside the house to do photo ops, and a Secret Service guy taps me on the shoulder and says, "I need to be where you are." "Okay."

So, we go inside the building, and he says, "Hey, that's [press secretary] Hope Hicks, she'll set you up with whatever you need." And I thought, "What in God's name am I . . . What am I going to do? This is not what I do." Anyway, so I spoke with Hope, who was just lovely and smart. I have met Trump, and people think that because I have met him that I can just call him. It is ridiculous. But the type of guy he is, which is what I enjoy about him and I like about him so much is that he is a guy. Just a guy from Queens, and I grew up in Brooklyn, so I get him. I get his humor all day long and he makes me laugh whenever I hear him speak.

So anyway, I get in there, and blah, this, and that, and this and that. And his line ends, and we go over to get in line, and the guy says, "He's done taking pictures." And Trump says,

"Get the hell out of the way and let my friends in." And we spoke with him for about . . . my wife and I, spoke with him for a few moments, and he was great. And I said, "Sir, whatever you need me to do." He says, "I'd like you to speak at the convention."

Baio at the Cleveland Convention

So then, I did not know what I would talk about, and somebody contacted me from the campaign. And he said, "Well, what are your thoughts?" I had a million of them, I landed on this one thing about making America great again, and all that.

Backstage, I was hanging out with Governor [Rick] Perry, and I am like, "Wait, what am I doing here?" And one of the guys that was running it says, "Hey, do you want to see the stage where you're going to be speaking?" It was empty, the convention center was empty, I went, "Sure." And he walked me out and I went, "Oh God."

Yeah, but it was empty. And I thought, "I can't. It is not what I do. I'm not a stand-up guy, I'm not a guy who gives speeches, or whatever." And I just completely got nervous and afraid. And then, I am waiting backstage, now the show's going on, and I am backstage with Willie from *Duck Dynasty* . . . Not Willie, oh God, forgive me. Anyway, I am back there with Rick Perry, and he and I are having a conversation, "And now, ladies and gentlemen, Scott Baio."

And I run out, and as soon as I hit the podium, I was fine. I just could not believe . . . I mean, I took it all in. It was amazing. It was one of the greatest moments.

I got a lot of pushback, as you can imagine. The pushback was, "Oh boy, look who Trump has at his convention, Scott Baio, and Antonio Sabato, and *Duck Dynasty* guys," and how pitiful all that was. And I would run into people that would say that to me to my face, and I would say, "Yeah, but we won, so maybe I helped him. You lost." And there was no way to go from there for them, which was quite enjoyable.

Saw Trump Next with Judge Jeanine

So, I started going on Fox News, and different news shows, and I was doing Judge Jeanine Pirro's show in New York, and she said, "Let us go do a man on the street thing from Trump Tower." "Sure." So, we went down there, and in walked [campaign manager] Corey Lewandowski. And he called Jeanine over and said, "Do you want to meet Mister Trump?" "Yeah." So, they put us in the bar and in he walks. And he is a big dude, I did not realize how big he is, he is a big guy.

And he walked in, he looked at me, he walked over to Judge Jeanine, gave her a big hug, turned to me and he says, "How are you doing?" I say, "Good." He said, "I won't forget what you did for me." I said, "Mister Trump, I don't want anything from you, I just want you to win." And we hung out for a few minutes.

Racism

And then came one of the questions I was asking before the George Floyd death: Is Donald Trump a racist?

Scott: No, he's not a racist. I do not even know . . . I know where it comes from, when he came down the escalator and said that people coming from Mexico are criminals, and some of them are. He did not say all of them, some of them are. And plus, he is loud, and he is brash, and they want the norm, they want it tied up tight, and locked in, and do not go off your script ever. And that ain't him. And I wish that Alyssa Milano, I really do, if she believes . . . I wish that all these actors out here, all of them, who are so anti-Trump, and so pro-liberal policies, would take their money, give it to the government, take in some illegals into their homes, do that, and then maybe I will believe you.

Blacklisting

It feels like *The Twilight Zone*. I am trying to think of the right adjective. It is infuriating that anybody can stop anybody else from working. And I have a huge problem with that. I am not a tough guy by any stretch of the imagination, but I will fight you. I will go down and you will go down, but I will fight you for stuff like that. That is not what we are. It is not what we are as a country, and liberals have made this their cause in Hollywood to not hire. And I know firsthand, and I know other people that are not being hired for certain things: camera guys, crew guys, because they are conservatives, and it happens all the time.

And I pray that one day this all . . . something happens, I do not know what, something happens. And I think Trump being elected is one of the things, he is exposing everything, all the crap that these people . . . all the corruption, lying, all of it, and I am hoping that . . . Everybody is so dug in, Daphne, everybody is so dug in on what they believe, and I do not even know who is an independent anymore, I really do not. If you are an independent, in my opinion, I do not think you have any idea what is going on. I think you are just an ignorant human being.

But I have just seen it, and it is heartbreaking for a lot of people. It is people who need the work. And something is going to happen, and Trump is going to expose something, and hopefully this will all flip. These news media are so horrible. I believe this. I believe that President Trump, him being elected was divine intervention. I believe that because I think this country . . . I am a Catholic boy from Brooklyn, I am not a conspiracy theorist, or I am not any weird . . . I'm just a black and white Brooklyn boy, but I think the way this country was going, this was intervention.

Invited to the White House

Scott might have lost jobs, got hurt . . . yet he was still invited to a White House Christmas party.

Scott: DC is great. I never went to the White House, which is just . . . We got invited there, whatever, and we have just been to the party, so it is in that sort of . . . not a huge area, little area. And you walk around, and it is just unbelievable. So, you could tell when the president's coming because there is a lot of move-ment going on, and a lot of Secret Service guys start . . . So, my wife takes me, and she pushes me up to the front of the crowd. I am sorry, she was waiting there, I was downstairs eating, so she waited at the front for like twenty [minutes] . . . And here comes the president and the first lady, and he is giving a speech. He is, and he is just whatever. She is stunning, lovely.

He comes up, and he makes . . . he says something, and then Billy Graham's son, Reverend Graham was there, he comes up and says something. And the president's looking at me, and he says, "I know he doesn't like to do this." And I go, "Yeah, I do. I'll do it." And he goes, "Oh, okay. Well, come on up, Scott Baio, here." And I got up and made a thirty-second speech. They push us off to the side.

And the president and the first lady are done, and he turns to about eight of us, and he turns to us and he goes, "Hey, you guys want to come to the Lincoln bedroom?" "Yeah." So, we go up, and the Secret Service guys are all around, and we go in the Lincoln bedroom and the president's there. By the way, what is interesting about him, when he is in the room, even when he was not president, he sucks up all the oxygen. I mean, he is a giant personality, I have never seen anything like it.

So, he is standing, and he says, "Lincoln's son died in this bed." And I said, "I'd forgotten about that." I think he had pneumonia. And then, over there is the desk where Abraham Lincoln wrote the Gettysburg Address, and there is the Gettysburg Address. And you go over to it, and there is the Gettysburg Address.

Oh, before we go into the Lincoln bedroom, you go up the stairs, to the right was the residence, to the left was the Lincoln bedroom, and we are standing and he goes, "Hey everybody, these are the residence." And he goes, "Nice, right?" And somebody goes, "Yeah, but it's not like Trump Tower." He goes, "No, but it's nice, right?" And we go to the Lincoln bedroom, he shows us everything. We must have been there for about fifteen minutes. And I kept calling the first lady Mrs. Trump, and my wife says, "You're not supposed to call her that." "So, what do you call her?" "The first lady." I went, "I don't think so."

So, she was standing, I said, "Can I ask you a question? Am I disrespecting you by calling you Mrs. Trump?" She goes, "No, that's my name. No, you're fine." And she could not have been nicer. So then, on the way out, my wife says, "Our daughter has a crush on Barron." And he goes, "Melania, we got another one." So, I said, "Mister President, can I give you a hug?" And I gave him a big hug, and I said, "Sir, I go to war with you." He goes, "I know it." And I left.

***

In 2021, even that innocent rhetoric, "I go to war with you," can get Scott Baio in trouble. It's troubling how growing American division is testing our basic freedom of speech.

#MeToo: Brett Ratner

At this stage, what does #MeToo have to do with this book?

Strangely—it does!

Simply because, the idiosyncrasies of Hollywood have not escaped anyone since the 2016 presidential elections.

For the perspective of this book, Brett Ratner became the odd man out of the two dozen interviewees.

He idiotically thought if he could just reappear in Hollywood as if nothing had happened. Maybe he read it in the Trump playbook: "Never Apologize!"

Like insisting being part of a documentary that would naturally remind everyone of the sexual allegations against him
would be a brilliant move?

For some reason, Brett was hoping to get great media attention for announcing his first directing project, the biopic of 1980s
musical group Milli Vanilli since he was forced to lay low after
being accused of sexual harassment by several actresses.

When the media found out, the reporters refreshed these
allegations.

Avi Lerner, another one of the twenty-four interviewees,
immediately putout a statement and came out clean that he and
his company are to disassociate themselves from Brett's project.

At last, there was unity!

A step closer to "One America."

#MeToo Movement

The #MeToo movement was actually created in 2006 by sexual harassment survivor Tarana Burke. But it became a powerful movement in late 2017 when both the *New York Times* and
the *New Yorker* exposed the massive accusations against Harvey
Weinstein.

From that moment on, actresses who have been terrified to
talk shared their stories of longtime sexual abuse in Hollywood.
Some of them were big names.

And many of the biggest names in Hollywood started to fall
down like a domino effect.

Nobody was too big for that movement: Like a tsunami, it
washed down everybody who was caught in it—heads of television networks and chief executive officers of studios, television
anchors who were receiving eight-figure salaries, and Hollywood
A-listers.

There is one word that Hollywood has traditionally wel-
comed: *comeback*.

How Many Oscar winners have been applauded for their "comeback" roles?

Yet, the new reality dictated new rules! None of the directors, executives, actors, or talents who lost their jobs or deals, being accused by the #MeToo healing culture, could make that Hollywood victorious comeback. Not one.

I have actress friends who have been victims of sexual harassment.

I supported Gretchen Carlson loudly when she sued then-Fox boss Roger Ailes, though she was badmouthed at the beginning.

This had nothing to do with my friendship with members of the Murdoch family (which came around later and gave justice to brave Gretchen).

Brett Ratner

When Brett Ratner's name came up while we were filming *Trump vs. Hollywood*, it made sense to me. He is a veteran director who scored some hits like the *Rush Hour* film series with Jackie Chan. I was the executive producer of *Jackie Chan Showing Hong Kong*, a successful Discovery Channel special.

Bill and I used to bump into Brett in Los Angeles or New York. We had mutual friends from the years I was filming with Michael Jackson and his parents.

Brett even introduced me to his Cuban-Jewish grandmother. Producer Avi Lerner told me that Brett and he talked about Avi taking part in our film.

Since we were already including a mega Hollywood attorney (Mark Geragos) and top producer (Lerner), why not a successful director?

I knew, of course, that there were accusations of sexual harassment against him. I knew that some in Hollywood wrote him off. Yet, Brett always denied the accusations. I did not recall that there was a trial. In the US, I believed, everyone is innocent until proven guilty.

The topics of the film, like divided America, racism, black-listing in Hollywood, politics and Hollywood, were very specific and I thought Brett would be an interesting interviewee.

He was. More eventful than any of us could predict. It started with a normal scheduling. In the middle of the night—a few hours before the filming—I heard my mobile getting texts.

It was Brett telling me about his grandmother being sick, asking me to postpone for couple of days. I called the hotel we were filming at as well as the film crew and canceled, explaining the urgent text.

It would become a ritual: Scheduling again, booking the film crew and hotel suite. Getting similar texts in the middle of the night.

At last—it happened. Brett wanted to film at his home. He told us that he has not left his home for a while due to COVID-19 and taking care of his grandmother.

He asked me for a favor: Would we agree that our film crew would also film him addressing a Chinese film festival that had invited him before COVID-19 took over? I did not see any problem.

Later that evening Bill and I had dinner with Jon Voight. Our cameraman Tim joined us, and told Jon about the many times Brett cancelled in the middle of the night. Jon was concerned.

I then remarked that thank God we were there to facilitate him recording his message to China. "I had to stop him from apologizing for not coming there due to COVID-19."

Jon was shocked. "COVID-19 came to us from China!" he exclaimed.

We called Brett together, worried, to check on him. We found Brett at his garage, where he wanted to film. He was sweating.

Bill was worried. During the COVID-19 spread, sweating might be anything.

Filming was interesting. Brett knows how to talk eloquently about Hollywood and its political ties. I liked some parts of it. His passion for making films was genuine.

The Hollywood Reporter Article

We would be in Washington, DC, when the film publicist scheduled an interview with the *Hollywood Reporter*. Bill and I just came back from a meeting at the West Wing with Jared Kushner, Trump's senior advisor and son-in-law.

The reporter, Chris Gardner, was very knowledgeable and the conversation went to familiar areas: Trump, Hollywood, politics.

Gardner remarked that Brett Ratner has not been seen for a while. That there have been these sexual harassment accusations.

I answered that as far as I was aware, Brett Ratner had not done any interviews since sexual misconduct allegations surfaced. Did he address his status in Hollywood?

Brett is a friend of mine and a friend of Avi and it was not about that. Our experience was quite different. He was very scared to do this interview not because of the allegations; he was scared to do the interview because of COVID. He does have his grandmother from Cuba living with him, and he is very devoted to her. Avi Lerner was also born in Israel. We are all what we call the Israeli mafia. He canceled it a few times because he did not know what to do.

But when we went to [interview] him, he was sweating. He was sweating and sweating, you will see in the film. Bill said, "Daphne, let us get the crew out, let us leave. He has COVID." I said, "No, he's sweating because he's nervous." It was very funny. I did not know the facts about [Ratner's misconduct allegations]. I am super supportive of #MeToo. Gretchen Carlson would tell you I am the one who supported her from day one. I have a remarkably close relationship with the Murdoch family. In everything, we have to know the facts. I do not know about

Brett; he is a friend. Everybody should be innocent until proven guilty. Brett is a lovable guy, very talented.

Raechal Shewfelt published an article in Yahoo! about our film, which included a link for the film trailer. It got more than seventy thousand clicks in a few hours.

Variety and other publications called our publicist. They all showed great interest to the documentary but they also asked about Brett Ratner!

All of a sudden I started getting endless text messages from Brett. Instead of thanking me for giving him benefit of the doubt, it included cursing, and threats. . . Some of them (many) came at the middle of the night.

Somebody brought to my attention his much-publicized texts, published in the *Hollywood Reporter*—the same pattern of endless irrational texts.

He told us he was planning a comeback.

Him being OUT (talking about other topics than his own accusations) brought back the #MeToo associated allegations, he ranted in language I cannot repeat.

I actually felt sad for him.

Anytime he came out, after these allegations, would bring them back.

You cannot hide from #MeToo.

So far, #MeToo had the total upper hand.

And then came the explosive media reports (*Vanity Fair*, the *Hollywood Reporter*, and other key outlets) that actress Charlotte Kirk sued to vacate the gag order that kept her silent about what described as sexual abuse by former Warner Brothers chief Kevin Tsujihara (who was ousted as a result) and others.

Brett Ratner's texts were all over the place.

The *Hollywood Reporter* reported that Ratner was served at his home. Did I say it before: You cannot hide from #MeToo?

These disturbing new articles came long after we filmed and started editing.

Their content about what allegedly happened and the reported deal to silence a woman, was hard to digest.

We needed to re-edit and leave Ratner on the cutting room floor.

CHAPTER SIX

Coming Home

Trump White House calling and African Americans are talking about their fears and anxieties!

Better yet, Black Lives Matter-supporting African Americans are entering into conference call with President Trump when he calls them from their home numbers!

E nough of Hollywood and all its idiosyncrasies, already!
It is the White House that matters in this country and the world, first and foremost.

Especially since Trump took over, most of the attention moved away from Hollywood even further, having sucked all the oxygen out of red carpets and awards ceremonies.

Promptly, when President Trump extended a hand recognizing the divide some of the most unlikely met him halfway. Despite everything, at the end, when the 2020 presidential elections were concluded, America was seeking normalcy somewhere else.

On that note, that is all the more reason why "one America" must be attained.

Trump Extended Hand

Yes, at the end of the journey, Daphne was able to get Black Lives Matter-supporting African Americans to talk with Donald J.

Trump, the forty-fifth president of the United States of America, on the phone.

Yes, they talked two days before the 2020 presidential elections and the White House released a press release inviting everybody on the conference call to celebrate Christmas at the White House.

Yes, the conference call lasted for a half-hour, and everybody was cordial. The encounter was enjoyable to all concerned and the invitation to celebrate Christmas together at the people's house was accepted by everyone on the line.

Yes, this project accomplished its goal of making the "divided America" "one America," at least during the phone call, as well as making the documentary and indeed during the Christmas celebration at the White House.

***

President Donald Trump made the historic call two days before the November 3 election at home and congratulated them. He talked to four people on the phone from Air Force One, parked on the tarmac.

Three rappers, one basketball player, one TV reality star, one soap opera celebrity, one comedian, and one assistant to President Trump became the highlight of this documentary. Their common ground was that they were African Americans.

Yet, going to the White House Christmas party was the most entertaining part of the whole thing. By then, President Trump was a no-show, understandably he was dealing with the result of the election, but everybody took the invite and cherished the job they all did in the people's house.

White House Calling

I was the "fourth" on the call, and the one that had orchestrated it.

The other three were part of the twenty-four, starring in the film Bill and I produced, *Trump vs. Hollywood: The Two White Houses*.

For Rallies and a Presidential Call

It was Saturday night, November 1, when an unlikely telephone call came to the homes of three African American public figures. It said: "This is the White House calling. . . Hold on for the President of the United States, Donald Trump!"

I was the "fourth" on the call, and the one that had orchestrated it. The other three were part of the twenty-four starring in the film Bill and I produced, *Trump vs. Hollywood: The Two White Houses*.

They were rapper Eric B, rapper Money B, who had founded Digital Underground with the late Tupac Shakur, and actor Isaiah Washington. Basketball player Glen (Big Baby) Davis was cut off the call due to bad weather in New Orleans.

It took a few seconds more, before Trump's familiar voice came on: "Hi, Daphne. How are you?"

I started to introduce the guys on the call, one by one, adding personal touch, in order to break the ice, after months of racial uprising following the death of George Floyd.

Trump was calling after appearing at four rallies two days before Election Day: the same challenging schedule that had brought him the surprising victory in 2016. Despite that, he was engaging and attentive.

I asked Eric B to remind the president that they had met thirty years ago in the company of Mike Tyson and Don King. The rapper dived into the colorful story and credited Trump at the end: "You told me: 'Eric, never be afraid, to hire smarter people than you.' I followed your advice, Mr. President."

Trump loved hearing that and returned the compliment: "AND what a successful career you have had."

I then teased Robert Brooks (Money B), telling Trump: "When we filmed, I asked Money B, what would he say to you, if you met for the first time. Money B's expression is changing in the movie, into a horrific one: "You want ME to talk with TRUMP?"

Money B explained that he agreed with me, that we must start to talk with each other and —though reluctantly—he agreed to this conversation and is looking forward to continuing it.

Then came Isiah.

Eric B talked about the need for "this uncomfortable conversation."

Keeping Air Force One on the Tarmac During the Call!

I kept monitoring, making sure that each had equal time with Trump, who invited us all "to the White House after the election." Trump, who was facing another two days of campaigning around the clock, was accommodating, and added "For YOU, I have time."

In fact, after almost a half-hour of conversation, I found a text from Jared Kushner, wondering how much more did I need? Apparently, Air Force One had landed during the conversation and everyone was sitting on the tarmac, waiting for Trump to finish talking with us.

The first step was accomplished. Jared and I started to work with our teams on a press release that both sides would agree reflected what just happened:

President Donald J. Trump Invites African American Stars to White House after Heart-to-Heart Conversation

LOS ANGELES, Nov. 2, 2020 /PRNewswire/ – Fighting 4 One America – A prominent group of African American actors and entertainers have accepted President Donald J.

Trump's invitation to visit the White House in December to work together on important issues facing the Black Community.

In a late-night night phone call with the President Saturday night, rappers Eric B and Money B, actor Isaiah Washington, who are among the stars in *Trump vs. Hollywood*, and film director Daphne Barak, all agreed to continue their discussion of economic opportunity, criminal justice reform and the President's groundbreaking "Platinum Plan" to deliver greater opportunity, security, prosperity and fairness to their communities.

"Thirty years ago, I had a conversation with Donald Trump, and he told me never to be afraid to hire the best people in business, even if they have more experience than me," said rap pioneer Eric B, a lifelong Democrat. "And that conversation has shaped my business decisions ever since. I am pleased that President Trump is willing to have this uncomfortable conversation about how we can help the black community close the wealth gap."

"President Trump took the time to get on the phone with us after a long day with four campaign rallies and I took that to mean he cares about our concerns," said Money B. "It's refreshing, and a good beginning. We want to get to work."

"I know firsthand what the Fake News media can do to a person, and I see what they keep trying to do to President Trump," said Isaiah Washington. "I'm now solidly with President Trump and I'm liking what I'm seeing in the results already."

"We filmed a documentary in real time during the pandemic, and with so much going on from the coronavirus to George Floyd, we wanted to hear from both sides of the political spectrum," said film executive producer and director Daphne Barak. "We spoke with a variety of celebrities and a common theme among many was *"Can we just talk?"* We are pleased that President Trump took time from his packed schedule to talk and listen. All people on the call felt that he really wants to have an open conversation with the Black community."

The artists had just completed a sneak preview of Barak's documentary, *Trump vs. Hollywood*, which is an examination of the divisions in America and an attempt to bring opposing ideologies together for a long-overdue civil discussion. Barak interviewed 24 Hollywood stars, musicians, rappers, and notable figures from both sides of the political spectrum during the pandemic about their candid feelings regarding President Trump and America.

In addition to Eric B, Money B, Isaiah Washington, and Glen "Big Baby" Davis, who was unable to join Saturday's call but will be joining the White House meeting in December, *Trump vs. Hollywood* includes: musician Kid Rock, vocalist Andrea Bocelli, actor Scott Baio, actor Dean Cain, actor Robert Davi, actress Kristy Swanson, actor Kevin Sorbo, actress and author Sam Sorbo, musician Ted Nugent, actor Eric Roberts, actress and casting director Eliza Roberts, director Brett Ratner, rapper Too Short (who has also been invited to the December meeting), producer Avi Lerner, Hollywood lawyer Mark Geragos, actor and reality star Claudia Jordan, actor and reality star Lorenzo Lamas, radio host Bill Whittle, and comedian DeRay Davis.

Trump vs. Hollywood premieres on December 14 across streaming platforms including Amazon, Apple TV, and Google. For a limited time, ahead of the election, a sneak preview of *Trump vs. Hollywood* is available for rent on Vimeo.

* * *

While Too Short had lunch with us and considered if he would like to talk to then-President Trump, his manager Arshia did talk to Trump's senior advisor Ja'Ron Smith on the phone. He decided at the end that he would wait until after the elections. Claudia Jordan was never invited to be a part of the conversation with President Trump. She comes out very strong and articulate in the film. Yet it was clear that they had a very personal falling out and, therefore, we did not suggest her name among those who have never met President Trump.

It Happened After I Asked Some Rappers if They Would Meet Trump

It all started several weeks before, when Bill and I were editing *Trump vs. Hollywood* with our team. People in the industry started to talk about how "inclusive" our film is, giving a platform to both sides of our divided country, and managing to show the deep pain crying to be heard.

When I pushed even the extreme interviewees, they at last agreed that we should all talk, or it will be too late for the sake of America. I asked some of the rappers if they would agree to talk with Trump, not only as a narrative of a film, but in reality.

It was in the spirit of reaching out. Start building bridges. I did not ask who they were voting for and repeated what I told Trump in our phone call: that whether he won or lost, he did represent half of the country, and these two halves must work together as one nation.

I then sent Jared Kushner, Trump's son-in-law and top advisor, an urgent text. He called me immediately back. It was an hour before the second debate between Trump and Joe Biden. The first debate had featured a "disruptive" Trump.

So, the second debate became almost crucial to his campaign. Still, Jared and I talked about the importance of creating such a direct ongoing conversation and not a two second photo op. We decided to meet at the White House in the next few days.

All hell broke loose after the meeting had been set up.

President Donald Trump and First Lady Melania got COVID-19. So did others at the White House, after a maskless event for Amy Coney Barrett, who was nominated by Trump to the Supreme Court to take the seat of the late Ruth Bader Ginsburg.

The West Wing was reportedly deserted. Trump was taken to the military hospital, and his chief of staff was reportedly briefing reporters off the record that his medical condition was worrisome.

But as Trump likes to surprise even people who are familiar with his surprising nature, he emerged from the hospital sooner than expected and went back to the Oval Office to resume his duties and continue his massive campaigning before the election.

Our meeting with Jared was put back on immediately: it was a priority.

Bill and I walked into the West Wing, as we had done several times before, just to find it almost empty. It felt like the aftermath of a storm.

West Wing Delivering

> President Trump has delivered for Black America record low
> unemployment, Opportunity Zones, criminal justice reform, historic
> funding for HBCUs, and the list goes on.
>
> —Ja'Ron Smith, deputy assistant to President Trump

Meeting in the West Wing and Ice Cube Dilemma

The ROTUS (receptionist of the United States), sitting at the entrance to the West Wing where she functions as a semi-hostess, was clearly happy to have two guests and was chitchatty.

Then we joined Jared, who introduced us to Brooks Rollins. "She worked with Rick Perry. We brought her from Texas," said Jared, who was joined by Ja'Ron Smith, an African American whom we would learn later on was the most senior African-American during the Trump Administration.

Ja'Ron would become close to us, and his journey before and inside the Trump White House, is historically important. Jared told us about their attempts to engage famous black Americans, to work with them. Names were thrown in the room. Among them, rapper Ice Cube.

Rapper Too Short, who was part of our cast, told me how he was taping a record with three other rappers—Ice Cube, Snoop Dog, and E-40—during the isolation due to COVID-19. After finishing the filming with Too Short, we continued our political chats with him and his partner, Arshia, over lunch at the famous Polo Lounge in Beverly Hills and over the phone. I would even put Arshia on the phone with Ja'Ron in order to explore possible dialogue. So Too Short and Arshia were following Ice Cube's political postings on social media, while working with him.

Ice Cube Asked to Meet Jared

What they did not know was how he had already been in deep talks with the Trump administration. Bill and I learned that the rapper reached out through his partner and asked to meet with Jared. Ja'Ron, who coordinated the secret meeting, grew up in Ohio admiring Ice Cube.

Meeting with him was personal to Ja'Ron, who told me that day at the West Wing, "Nobody knows. . . We have been in communication with Ice Cube for thirty weeks by now." The rapper and the President's son-in-law met discreetly at the Willard Hotel next to the White House. The level of sensitivity during the racial uprising was very high.

For that reason, Jared, Ja'Ron, Bill, and myself decided to keep all communications regarding "building bridges" confidential and to ensure the rappers would not be condemned by their fans, just for agreeing to talk.

Indeed, when Ice Cube would admit later on that he was trying to work with the Trump administration, he created a storm. He tried to defend himself, that he had reached out to both Trump's and Joe Biden's campaigns, and while Biden's people preferred to wait until after the election, Trump's people (Ja'Ron) understood the important opportunity.

Ice Cube also professed that the black community needed to work with whomever was in power. He had a point. But the backlash was alarming.

It made others think and to weigh the side effects carefully.

Painful Moments with African American Interviewees

Too Short, whose painful interview in the film moved me (and early viewers) to tears, had been listening to my strong belief that he should talk to what he considered, "the other side"—Trump.

As much as he denounced Trump's rhetoric and behavior, Too Short, Arshia, and I were considering the benefits of reaching out to him.

Yet, Ice Cube's coming out and revealing a little about his sincere communication with the Trump team and being questioned by some loyal followers, made Too Short suggest: "Let us wait until after the elections."

In an atmosphere of such hatred, pain, frustration, how could I push him further?

I respected his honesty and understood that my big conviction to make "two Americas" talk may have to be done by taking "baby steps" and enduring some setbacks along the way.

Money B

Sometimes we feel that we need to take a brave step despite what those close to us or followers might say. A step we would not even consider only short time ago. That is what impressed me about Money B.

Hosting him and his father for lunch, witnessing the admiration and love he had for his former Black Panther dad, I had a glimpse of how out of the question it was for his immediate support group to digest an interaction with Donald Trump.

He would later share with me conversations with his stepmother after she heard about our phone call with Trump. She was loving, but cautioned him to hold on to his key values.

His wife was supportive, but worried. Money B is a curious, intelligent artist, who likes to explore, even if it was such a new and risky avenue for his traditional family and fans.

He told me seriously: "To go to the White House and hold in-depth conversation with Trump, Jared. Sure! It is important, what we established. But to go with Trump to a Christmas party? Oh no. It is way too early, before we achieve something."

I said that the White House is the house of the people and all Americans should be invited to see the great decorations and feel proud.

Naturally, these annual invitations are much sought after. I have been bombarded for years by friends or "friends of friends" who were nearly begging me to somehow take them with me, cause they MUST be seen there.

Not that it has been in my power. The invitees are usually big donors or friends or high- profile supporters of the current occupant of the White House. Money B, like others in my small group, felt great about being invited. Yet, he kept debating the optics of "partying with President Trump."

Glen "Big Baby" Davis, who had his own painful remarks about Trump's mistreating the black community, said: "I would cut [off] my arm if I miss this opportunity." For a basketball player, this is quite a statement. But history has the last laugh.

On November 3—two days after I introduced these passionate guys to President Trump— he lost the election. Early, on November 4, Trump appeared furious and started his big campaign claiming that the election was stolen.

From that moment on, the wall between the two Americas grew even taller:

Half of America were celebrating Joe Biden's victory with the first-ever woman vice president-elect, let alone, a Black and Indian woman. The other half—fueled by Trump's tweet-storms—believed that the Democrats stole the election and created a slogan, "Stop the Steal" which led to angry demonstrations, conspiracy theories, and a tsunami of social media posts.

Ja'Ron!

Ja'Ron Smith left the Trump administration on November 6. Here is one of media reports, from *The Hill*:

> Ja'Ron Smith, the highest-ranking Black person in the White House and a top aide who worked with Jared Kushner, left his position Friday.

A White House official confirmed that Smith had left his position and said his departure was long planned, regardless of the outcome of the election. The development was first reported by Bloomberg News.

Smith served as deputy assistant to President Trump for domestic policy and was first brought into the White House in 2017 to advise the president on urban affairs and revitalization policy. He became the highest-ranking Black individual in Trump's White House following the departure of Omarosa Manigault Newman in 2018.

In a lengthy statement issued later Friday, Smith said it was the "honor of a lifetime" to serve in the Trump administration and called his departure "bittersweet."

"When joining the Trump Administration, I set out to achieve the empty promises of the past, and I am proud to say promises made, promises kept. In four years, President Trump has delivered for Black America; record low unemployment, Opportunity Zones, criminal justice reform, historic funding for HBCUs, and the list goes on," Smith said.

"This decision was made in consultation with my family (one that will be growing very soon with the addition of twins) and given the blessing of my beloved colleagues at the White House long before the election," he said.

His departure comes three days after Election Day and as Democratic nominee Joe Biden appears on the verge of winning the presidential race after overtaking Trump in Georgia and Pennsylvania. Trump has insisted he will win reelection and plans to contest the results in some states."

"Daphne, I am still going to be committed to continue what we started with your film stars," Ja'Ron professed. "You will call Jared about the White House invitations for them, and I would talk with him too. I agree, it is so important."

He meant every word of it, and would become close to Bill and me.

"Stolen Elections"

Meanwhile, Trump, everybody would find out, could not be bothered about anything else but reversing what he considered "stolen elections."

When he saw me at one of his clubs, he greeted me, and said, "How nice you look," before an elderly woman pushed towards him. My friends were shocked witnessing how she literally promised him, "I am working for Johnny . . . You will see! You will win! Then she shouted a name of one of Trump's employees, who had been fired before, but was brought back, "He says that you will be the president another four years."

And Trump, a real savvy guy who hates to waste time, actually stopped and listened to these worthless screams. Because it was what he wanted to hear and people knew better than to tell him differently.

I told Ja'Ron that we really needed to ensure some serious conversation between Trump and some of the film stars, as had been agreed, in our telephone call. Ja'Ron confirmed what the mainstream media reported: The president was devoting his entire time and attention to trying to reverse the election's results.

He suggested I reach out to Trump. Though I had access to him, I knew better.

On With the Christmas Invitations

Meanwhile, the Christmas invitations started to come for Bill and I and our group.

In the spirit of the film, I decided to add two Trump supporters that appeared in the film to our group. I chose Kevin and Sam Sorbo, since they mentioned to us how they would appreciate an invitation from the president, whom they have been backing so loudly.

Sam Sorbo and Money B had already made their acquaintance when they both appeared with me on Pastor Greg Young's radio show, *Chosen Generation*, promoting the film and again on Annie Ubelis's radio show, joined by Ted Nugent's wife, Shemane.

I added our dear friend Bettina Viviano, who helped us book a couple of the conservative stars, and her husband Jimmie. To complete the festive group, I invited Dran Reese, a well-known conservative activist and donor, who brought her daughter Marley.

I cautioned Money B: "The rest of the group are true MAGA people. Let us all enjoy each other." He got it.

Celebrating Christmas at the White House

"No, I will not approach a cop and say: 'I have a reservation in this five star hotel, would you allow me to pass through the blockade?'"

—Well-known African American rapper
in Washington, DC, in 2020

At the Willard in Washington, DC

On Saturday, December 12, 2020, there was a major pro-Trump demonstration rally in Washington, DC. To some, after many drinks, it meant that no African Americans needed to be downtown.

Surely, this could have been a figment of someone's imagination but not to this particular African American. He needed to be there that day. He had to make it from Reagan National Airport to the Willard InterContinental Hotel in downtown Washington.

On that Saturday, a simple fifteen-minute taxi ride was impossible. If the patron was an African American, it was even a dangerous task. Was he pushing his luck with a wife, young kid, and elderly father back home waiting quarantined at home because of COVID-19?

No, none of that. He was there by the invitation of the forty-fifth president of the United States of America. His hosts were Daphne Barak and Erbil Gunasti, the director and the producer of the *Trump vs. Hollywood* documentary he was starring in, alongside twenty-three other equally famous Americans.

His problem was that the airport he landed and the hotel he was going to stay were on opposite ends of the divided city. A MAGA rally was underway and unless someone was a Trump supporter, there was no reason to be in this area until it was over.

There were two problems for an African American in Washington DC, during a MAGA rally. First, there were too many pro-Trump MAGAs in town. Worse, there were lots of police officers too.

So, Erbil decided to take this matter into his own hands. He told Daphne that he was going to go out, locate their guest, and personally walk him the ten or twenty blocks to the hotel.

Erbil knew their guest was going to be in trouble if he walked into a wrong crowd. More importantly, their guest had already told him that he was equally worried about the police officers.

Erbil did not think that was a problem, but nonetheless he had already started to think what his guest meant. When he walked out of the Willard, the immediate avenues and streets were empty. Law enforcement was everywhere.

He communicated with his guest, who had already left his Uber and was walking with his luggage, over the phone. They met and walked the rest of the way together.

***

Only an hour earlier, Daphne and Erbil had tracked a similar path to the same hotel. When their taxi eventually hit the police roadblock after circling the city for an hour, Daphne jumped out and approached the cop.

After whatever she explained, as a blonde American, the taxi was on its way to the front door of the Willard without any hassle. Later, they would learn that none of their guests would be as lucky. They would be walking to the Willard, rolling their luggage.

***

While unpacking, Money B called Bill. He told him that he just landed and was heading to the hotel. Bill told him what to do. Half an hour later, he called again. The streets were blocked. . . Cops were looking at his Uber. . . No! He was not going to exit the Uber. No, he was not going to approach the police for no reason!

In America, in 2020, a known African American musician was scared to approach a cop and say: "I have a reservation in this five-star hotel, would you allow me to pass through the blockade?"

***

Bill not only walked Money B to the hotel, but also suggested that they should go out and have a beer with all the MAGA people around.

When they returned with enough beers consumed few hours later, Money B had lots of interesting stories to tell. He passed them along to his followers through his Instagram account.

At Harry's Bar a few blocks from the hotel, Money B had apparently made friends because these MAGAs turned out to be fans of his famous songs, like "The Humpty Dance." They were so thrilled to have met him. Money B was also pleased to take pictures with them.

All the while, Bill was hard at work telling people that Money B was no friend of MAGA. His efforts were futile. No one cared. Nothing other than good company, beer, and food mattered.

Pro-Trump Bond with Rappers

The next day, Bill and I hosted a "welcome reception" for our group.

Kevin Sorbo was already spotted in the hotel lobby by fans. He was posing for photos, while wife Sam hugged Bettina and Dran. Even if they had not met before, they knew each other. That is common in the Trump world, which excites people to join groups, work for conservative media or advocate groups.

Money B was observing this. We mingled and then—it was party time! The first White House Christmas Party was about to start. Bill and I led Bettina and [her husband] Jimmie. Others would head to the next one that day.

The question in the air was: "Would *he* attend?"

On Friday, two days before, Trump, who had honestly believed that he could reverse the election's official results, suffered a deadly setback. The Supreme Court, which is one-third Trump appointees, rejected a lawsuit spearheaded by the state of Texas (joined by seventeen GOP states) to challenge the results in several states where Joe Biden won.

The president was reportedly so upset that he snubbed his own Christmas party at his own White House and was a no-show. Knowing Trump, I figured that he would no longer host any of the remaining Christmas parties.

As the smart man he is, he knew on Friday night that his second term as the President of the United States was not going to happen. He might have continued to energize his base and seemed to listen to "conspiracy theory experts," but deep down, he checked out from the White House that night.

Yet, Bettina and Jimmie were really looking forward to seeing him. As we walked into the reception, the band was playing festive music. The decorations were beautiful. So many Christmas trees. Dan Scavino, Trump's busy social media director, came over and took photos. Weeks later, Trump would be banned from social media.

The food was beef, spinach, desserts. . .The hit was the lamb chop counter. People lined up to have access to it. Kevin Sorbo managed to steal the attention of the next party. With no Trump in sight, guests elbowed to have photos with the *Hercules* actor.

The next day, it was time for Money B to enter the Trump White House.

Party at the Czech Republic House

Bill and I asked our friend, Hynek Kmonicek, the Czech Republic ambassador to the US, and his Bohemian wife, Indira, to host our group in their fascinating residence.

Hot Czech wine and endless Champagne were offered, while Kevin and Sam were inspecting the dead animals (and the guns!) on the walls.

Money B bonded with the artistic Indira, relaxing for his big night. At this point, he knew that Trump would not be at his own party. But who else from Trump's close circles would be there?

Apparently everybody.

Back to Christmas at the White House . . .

As Money B and I walked in, we bumped into Texas Governor Greg Abbott.

He and the Texas GOP were most supportive of Trump. He had visited the West Wing earlier that day. We chatted about our film and took photos, refraining from mentioning anything controversial in the news.

A woman joined us and introduced herself as the wife of one of Trump's lawyers during the impeachment. A perfect time to go upstairs and see more decorations. "Hey Daphne!" screamed a happy man, hugging me. Andrew Hughes, Ben Carson's chief of staff. He tells Money B and I that he had COVID-19 and shares how bad Carson's COVID-19 got.

Then, we touch the "No Touch" zone: "What are you going to do after January 20th?" A normal question during transitions of power, but a forbidden one this time around.

They told many political appointees not to look for jobs or they would be fired, Andrew and I whisper. Unlike others, Andrew, who introduces his lovely pregnant wife, tells us: "*Really?* So, I would lose three salaries?"

This kind of whispering would continue the rest of this glitzy evening.

Next we see Mark Meadows, Trump's chief of staff. I introduce him with his official title to Money B. We take photos. Then, while we dig into that lamb, Meadows reappears, takes me aside and says: "Let me give you my private number."

"You mean, after. . .?" I asked without pronouncing the inevitable. "Take it. Write it down now," he says and disappears.

Meadows would emerge, cheering with Donald Trump Jr., in a video streamed by the latter a few minutes before armed extremists stormed the Capitol and threatened the vice president and the Speaker of the House, resulting in the deaths of five people, shocking the nation.

An image which would become part of American history.

The Last Supper–like Party

A few steps away I introduce Money B to Mark Short, the chief of staff for VP Mike Pence. We take smiling photos as well. This would be probably the last party these two chiefs of staff will both attend.

Soon enough, Trump would tell his base, that *only Pence could reverse the election.* Talking with Short on the phone, I knew that Pence knew the Constitution did not give him such power, and he was going "to do the right thing." But Trump's massive pressure continued.

At the end, after a mob of angry MAGA supporters broke into the capital, some threatening to harm Mike Pence, Short found himself hidden from them with Pence and his family. Yeah. Shortly after Meadows was seen celebrating at the tent, with people who egged the crowd to "Go, FIGHT."

The next day, Mark Short would not be allowed to enter the White House, where the vice president's office is. But on December 14, a few weeks before, the chiefs of staff, top aides, are all mingling.

The next one we meet is Stephanie Grisham, the chief of staff to the first lady. Stephanie, who was the White House press secretary until Mark Meadows replaced her, is much prettier in person. We have met before at Mar-a-Lago. She takes genuine interest in Money B and understands how a big step it was for him to accept this invitation.

She shares with me that this would be the first time she would not spend Christmas in Mar-a-Lago in five years. She is walking the fine line of understanding that the Trump presidency was over without spelling it out.

Later, on January 6, she would be the first senior White House aide to resign following the bloodshed at the Capitol. "I didn't want the first lady to convince me to stay, as happened before," she tells Bill and I over lunch, "So I sent my resignation via email."

Before we exit what would become the Trump administration's "last supper," I hear my name being called out. Sean Spicer, the first White House press secretary, who cemented his place in American history at his first press briefing, by declaring: "It (the Trump inauguration) was the biggest crowd, PERIOD."

I like Sean. Bill and I famously plugged him on the *Extra* TV show, convincing friends Lisa Gregorisch-Dempsey, Theresa Coffino, and Jeremy Spiegel that he could do some political couples' interviews.

We supervised his segments with Mike and Susan Pompeo, Sarah Sanders and her husband, and Kellyanne Conway and her family.

Sean, who has a daily talk show on Newsmax, did not have to worry about what was coming next.

He posed for photos with Money B, and was more worried about, "Where is Bill?" than anything.

He had left the administration early enough to continue benefiting from it.

His network, Newsmax, was gaining more and more MAGA viewers, who left Fox News, per Donald Trump's angry tweets during the last several months, and more so after the election.

Another proof that Trump supporters are not going to dissolve any time soon. America is divided by growing emotions. And—can we just talk?

Money B cannot resist, doing a live Instagram from the White House to his astonished fans. Some of the party's guests crowded around us, smiling. Trying to get into the frame. Trump's big donors and Money B at the same frame. Laughing.

Seeking Normalcy with Biden

Irrespective of the track record of his predecessor, in the end Joe Biden was elected the forty-sixth president of the United States of America.

America was seeking normalcy. Some were finding it in Joe Biden.

Yet not everyone was sure that he was going to be the resident of the White House at 1600 Pennsylvania Avenue until January 20, 2021 when he entered the premises. He had to wait for the previous tenant to leave the place earlier in the morning on the same day to find out.

Why Joe Biden was elected and how the prospect of having the two White Houses suddenly appeared in horizon have become the most pertinent questions. Yet, neither side on this debate will have the right answers by the time this book will be published.

Why Joe Biden Was Elected

Joe Biden was not an odds-on favorite to win the Democratic primaries, yet as soon as COVID-19 descended upon America like a plague, he became the frontrunner who never relinquished the lead.

For Trump supporters, the prospects were no different in the 2020 elections than when Hillary Clinton was ahead in polls four years earlier. This time Democrat candidate Joe Biden did not fail and won the race and on January 6, 2021, when the results were certified.

Even then, the questions lingered. Today, when the transfer of power has long been consummated, no concession came from the losing side. America is in limbo at best, giving the benefit of doubt to the Biden Administration to deliver.

The Two White Houses

Meanwhile there is nothing left to do for the rest of America but to ponder the two White Houses. Here are some of the historical facts. They range from geography to philosophy to social issues to tragedies. They show eerie similarities.

1. For a four-year period in American history during the Civil War, two official houses carried the name White House. Standing ninety miles apart, across the Virginia landscape, one overlooked the Potomac River and the other the James.

2. The two presidents had some things in common, and much that they did not share. One thing certain: they did share commitment to their points of view. Both firmly believed that the paths they had taken would have been approved by the founding fathers.

3. Inside both presidential houses, the dynamics behind the scenes were directed forward in a smooth public presentation. Backstage all was by no means calm at the White House in Washington. Well before he went to the White House, Abraham Lincoln was concerned that all ceremonial activities be conducted properly. In Richmond, social responsibility was an easier matter for the first lady of the Confederacy, Varina Howell Davis. President Jefferson Davis took no part in planning anything, so capable was his wife.

4. Both the Lincolns and the Davises lost sons in their respective White Houses. Willie Lincoln died in the Lincoln bedroom, on February 20, 1862, probably of typhoid. In the spring of 1864, Joseph Davis II, age five, out of sight of his nurse and siblings, climbed on the railing of the rear porch and attempted to walk across it, like a trapeze artist he had admired at the circus. He fell on the brick terrace below and crushed his skull.

Since half of America is into cancel culture, No-No rhetoric, and wants nothing to do with history anymore, there is nothing to ponder by looking back.

Rather it is now high time for struggling for one America.

Since everything is bleak in the back, it is time to look forward, maybe on a new page.

For now, if only, we could just freeze this moment and add: "END."